The
One to One
Manager

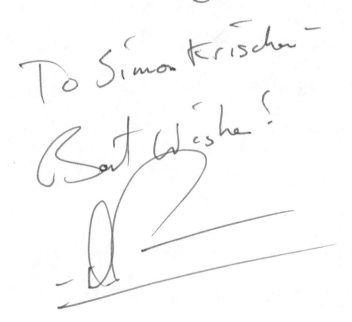

To Simon Krischen—

Best Wishes!

Also by Don Peppers and Martha Rogers

Enterprise One to One

The One to One Future

The One to One Fieldbook
(co-authored with Bob Dorf)

The
One to One
Manager

**Real-World Lessons in
Customer Relationship Management**

Don Peppers and Martha Rogers, Ph.D.

CURRENCY

DOUBLEDAY

New York London Toronto Sydney Auckland

A Currency Book

published by doubleday

a division of Random House, Inc.

1540 Broadway, New York, New York 10036

Currency and Doubleday

are trademarks of Doubleday, a division of Random House, Inc.

Book design by Chris Welch

Library of Congress Cataloging-in-Publication Data

Peppers, Don.

The one to one manager: real-world lessons in customer

relationship management / Don Peppers and Martha Rogers. — 1st ed.

p.   cm.

Includes index.

1. Customer relations—Management. 2. Consumers' preferences.

3. Relationship marketing.   I. Rogers, Martha, Ph.D.   II. Title.

HF5415.5.P46   1999

658.8′12—dc21   99-26835

CIP

ISBN 0-385-49408-4

The One to One Manager is dedicated
to General Robert McDermott,
a trailblazer and pathfinder.

Contents

Contents

Contents

Acknowledgments

Over the course of researching and writing *The One to One Manager,* we were blessed with the cooperation and assistance of many fine friends. We would like to honor these friends now and express our gratitude for the support and insight they so willingly gave. We thank our agent, Rafe Sagalyn, and our publisher, Roger Scholl, for their belief in us and for their unswerving commitment to this project. We are indebted to Pem McNerney, David De Long and Frances Jones for reading early drafts of the manuscript and offering constructive criticism that was both wise and incalculably helpful. Among our colleagues at Peppers and Rogers Group, we thank Christine DiGrazia, Ben Kunz, Mary Cavello, Deanna Lisk, Stratos Kontargyris, Faisal Khan, Nichole Clarke, Stacey Riordan, Tony Kubrin and Brian Roberts. Extra thanks to Josh Stailey, for tireless effort and extremely useful advice.

We owe a special debt of gratitude to Mike Barlow, our editorial director, who kept the project on track from start to finish. A great writer and editor in his own right, Mike did a wonderful job in pulling together the interviews, extracting the stories, and boiling them down to their essential issues. We could not have completed this book on time without Mike's help. In fact, without Mike we couldn't have completed the book at all. Thanks, Mike!

The One to One Manager is really a series of stories that "belong" to the many subjects we interviewed. For their time and attention, and for their critical eye, we thank the "pioneers" of one-to-one marketing who agreed to talk to us and share their stories with our readers. Thanks to Dick Vague, Dr. Paul Otte, John Samuel, Gustavo Covacevich, Gordon Shank, Janie Ligon, Jim McCann, Jack Antonini, General Robert McDermott, Patrice Listfield, Patrick J. Kennedy, Anne Lockie, Shauneen Bruder, Steve Wiggins, Brenda French, Bruce Varner, Marc Breslawsky, Richard Costello, Klaus Huber, Shirley Choy-Marshall, Shen Li, Dr. Jim Goodnight, Pamela Meek, Doug Mello, Ken Robb, Caroline Dennis, Stephen Cannon, Woody Harford, Silvio Bonvini, Katrina Garnett, Nina Smith, Paul Allaire, Tracy Faleide, Pam McGee, Kevin O'Connor, Neil Mendelson and Jim Poage. We salute these pioneers, for their vision, courage and endurance.

Most of all, however, we thank our spouses, Pamela Devenney and Stuart Bertsch, for once again putting up with what has by now become a familiar series of missed weekends, 5 A.M. writing sessions and deadline-driven crankiness. We are both truly blessed.

—*Don Peppers and Martha Rogers, Ph.D.*

The
One to One
Manager

Preface

In 1993 we introduced the idea of "one-to-one market-ing" in our book, *The One to One Future: Building Relationships One Customer at a Time.* This book represented our attempt to describe a brand-new type of competition and to persuade readers that one-to-one marketing (also referred to as customer relationship management, or CRM) is worth considering as a strategy for keeping customers loyal and protecting unit margins.

In 1997 we wrote a second book, *Enterprise One to One: Tools for Competing in the Interactive Age.* In that book we tried to flesh out the theory of one-to-one marketing, examining the types of business situations where it was appropriate. We argued that one-to-one marketing is actually a competitive strategy going far beyond the word "marketing." Success in this discipline, we said, would require the active participation and support of a variety of functions at the enterprise, including not just sales and marketing, but production, information technology and channel management as well.

In early 1999 we wrote *The One to One Fieldbook: The Complete Toolkit for Implementing a 1to1 Marketing Program* (coauthored with Bob Dorf, president of Peppers and Rogers Group). The *Fieldbook,* with its voluminous and detailed checklists and action steps, was a comprehensive effort to document the "how to" issues involved in one-to-one marketing. Linked to a continuously updated, password-protected Web site containing case studies and self-help tools, the *Fieldbook* was the third book in a trilogy about the origins, theory and practice of one-to-one marketing.

The One to One Manager is both our fourth book about one-to-one marketing and our first book in a new series—a series designed to document real-world stories of one-to-one marketing. *The One to One Manager* examines the actual management issues involved in implementing CRM initiatives, relying exclusively on more than two dozen case histories from around the world. We believe this book is a natural first step in the new series. But even as it goes to press we are already at work on the next installment in the series, *The One to One Sales Force.* Following that, we plan to tackle issues such as systems integration, human resources and World Wide Web strategies.

One-to-one marketing is still a new enough idea that few people really know what to expect. Interpreting results can be difficult. Anticipating—and dealing with—the inevitable snags and problems that arise as one-to-one initiatives are introduced can be frustrating. For those of you who are moving forward with CRM programs, it's important to remember that you're not alone. This new series of *One to One* books will document the successes—and failures—of the one-to-one marketing revolution.

These books will tell the real stories of the men and women who are now implementing CRM programs all over the world. And, in all honesty, it's a blast researching these mini-case histories (or "caselets," as we call them). We pick up a tremendous amount of valuable information to share with you, and it is educational for us too. In every case, our goal is to offer enough information for you to draw practical lessons from these stories—lessons that can help you avoid pitfalls and maximize opportunities.

But if there's one thing that should become clear beyond doubt as you read through this book, it is that the ideas and concepts that make up the discipline of one-to-one marketing are here to stay. This is not a fad. This is the reality of today's competitive landscape. The "one-to-one future" is no longer the future. It's happening now.

We're looking forward to continuing this journey of exploration with you. Thanks for your continued support.

Introduction

Hungry Dragons

In the business world, what might be called the Era of Mass Marketing has now entered the twilight, and the sun is rising on a new age. Whether we choose to call this new period the "Age of Interactivity" or the "Era of Customer Relationship Management," one thing is certain: The landscape under our feet is being transformed radically. Is there anyone who doubts that customer expectations have risen—and are continuing to rise—dramatically? Is there anyone who sees this trend reversing itself? Is there anyone who still dismisses the World Wide Web as marginal?

If you are reading this book, chances are you're already well aware of the tidal forces now reshaping the global economy, and you're looking for answers. You might be wondering how to harness new technologies to deal with your customers' rising expectations. Maybe you're concerned about managing the turbulence of the organizational changes you must make to stay competitive.

These are the kinds of questions and concerns plaguing all thinking business people today. The important thing is not to let them deflect you from your path.

Let's begin by asking a question: Why is all this happening *now?*

The convergence of the Baby Boomer ethos ("I want it the way I want it and I want it now!") and the rapidly dropping cost of information technology has resulted in a genuine cultural earthquake. Unlike the "revolution" of the 1960s, which generated more light than heat, this revolution is indelibly changing the way we all live. Perhaps the strangest aspect of this revolution is that so few people seem to notice that it's happening. Yet within the next few years many of our basic assumptions about commerce and industry will be overturned. Commonly held notions about privacy and security will be severely tested, if not discarded outright.

The revolution we are talking about is the one-to-one marketing revolution—a technology-driven movement that is now affecting, in one way or another, virtually every business, in every industry, all around the world.

Make no mistake: Managers at every level will be affected. The fortunate ones will get support for those changes from the top. Others will be faced with the daunting task of educating up the hierarchy. Only the very lucky will escape wrestling over issues such as institutional resistance, lack of effective communication and misunderstandings about the role of technology.

Why? Because the whole idea of technology-enhanced relationship management is so new and untested, any company making progress in this discipline can easily find itself in totally new territory, where there are few precedents and little to hold on to in terms of accepted wisdom or tried-and-true practices.

Remember those ancient world maps decorated with hungry dragons and depicting a flat earth composed mostly of "Terra Incognita"? Well, that's where we are now. And don't be fooled. There are dragons waiting to eat us if we don't master the strategies necessary to keep us from falling off the edge of the world.

Scouts, Pathfinders and Navigators

A new era, like a new continent, requires explorers: people of intelligence, vision, courage and resilience moving forward into the unknown, driven by curiosity and enlightened self-interest to discover, map and demystify the wilderness. In this book we'll visit with scouts, pathfinders and navigators committed to exploring and taming the new territory ahead. We'll share their experiences and observations, and listen to their firsthand accounts from the skirmish lines.

Think of this book as a book of messages, sent back to us from the uncharted frontier of one-to-one marketing and customer relationship management (CRM), by some of the most accomplished and successful pioneers in the territory. They are letting us know what it's like out there. Some of them, no doubt, are destined for celebrity status—at least in business circles—for their contributions to this new age. A few of them already *are* legendary, such as General Robert McDermott. In the early 1970s, McDermott used the most modern computer technology available to remake a stodgy, paperwork-infested, bureaucratic insurance company, USAA, into what has become one of the most persuasive success stories of relationship marketing.

Or consider Richard Vague, the innovative CEO of First USA Bank, who suggests that the most important thing his bank can do today is become the "trusted agent" of its customers. To do this, Vague has created a concierge-like program that is fed by the Internet but delivered to most of his customers by phone.

"Trusted agent." Remarkably similar, if not identical, words are used by several of the other executives we interviewed for this book. Dr. Paul Otte uses the same concept in explaining his efforts to shape a one-to-one college education experience at Franklin University in Ohio. Royal Bank of Canada's Anne Lockie is so committed to applying this concept to each of her bank's nine million customer relationships that she set up a branch office in a rural dairy barn so her bankers could work face-to-face with local customers.

We will hear from Brenda French of French Rags, who has created one of the world's premier lines of custom clothing for women by relying on a visionary application of mass customization technology. Kevin O'Connor, founder of DoubleClick, invented a unique management method to ensure that critical business decisions affecting customer relationships aren't made in a vacuum.

Marc Breslawsky, president of Pitney Bowes, will explain how his company launched an internal revolt to disrupt a pattern of complacency and replace it with a service mentality. Patrice Listfield, a division president at Southern New England Telephone (now itself a division of SBC), will guide us through the complexities of integrating customer management across different business units serving an overlapping customer base. Jack Antonini of First Union will talk to us about how he reorganized his bank's consumer businesses to improve customer retention and increase long-term profitability. Jack got his one-to-one marketing training by working alongside General McDermott at USAA.

Shirley Choy-Marshall, a manager at Hewlett-Packard's HP Shopping Village online store, will shed light on channel issues that can arise when a product-centric firm launches a customer-friendly Web site.

Steve Wiggins, the founder and former CEO of Oxford Health Plans, will speak candidly about the difficulty of keeping culture and technology in synch. Katrina Garnett, CrossWorlds Software's high-profile "CEO in the black velvet dress," will talk about her effort to put a human face on her company, so her customers could relate more personally to a firm offering such a complex product. Gordon Shank, chief marketing officer at Levi Strauss, will explain the past and future of his organization's much-heralded mass customization effort. Gustavo Covacevich, CEO of Previnter, one of Argentina's largest pension management firms, will tell us how he re-engineered a common electronic gadget to help his sales people stay focused on their customers and compete more effectively.

We'll touch base with other one-to-one managers as well. We'll hear from executives at large and small organizations alike, from the Carrollton, Texas, fire department to Xerox; from British Airways to SAS Institute.

Many of the managers and executives you'll meet in this book are people whose ideals and sensibilities were forged in the 1950s and 1960s. As a group, they tend to be more thoughtful, more empathetic and more people-focused than their predecessors, whose values and behaviors were shaped during the Depression and World War II. Empowered by the technological advances of the 1990s, these new managers are the leaders whose worldview will shape the first decade of the twenty-first century.

But before we delve too deeply into the stories brought to us by these pioneers, let's define the nature of this new type of competition, and then outline some of the principles that underlie success in the new territory.

What Is "One-to-One Marketing"?

The One to One Manager is the fourth in our series of "one-to-one" titles. We hope you're already acquainted with the first three—*The One to One Future: Building Relationships One Customer at a Time* (1993); *Enterprise One to One: Tools for Competing in the Interactive Age*

(1997) and *The One to One Fieldbook: The Complete Tool-kit for Implementing a 1to1 Marketing Program* (1999, coauthored with Bob Dorf). In this series of books we have laid out a completely new "theory" for competing in the post-industrial age, and we've documented our work with a large number of examples from around the world.

It doesn't really matter what we call this new competitive idea, now sweeping through boardrooms and dominating business planning everywhere. We've called it "one-to-one marketing," or simply "1to1." Others have created alternate terms, such as customer relationship management (CRM), enterprise relationship management (ERM), customer intimacy, real-time marketing, continuous relationship management and technology-enabled relationship marketing, among others. The idea appears in many guises, but it is a singular idea nonetheless, based on developing and managing individual relationships with individual customers.

A relationship, of course, is made up of a continuing series of collaborative interactions. Because it goes on through time, a relationship develops a "context," as both parties to it—the company and the customer—participate in successive interactions. And each relationship is different, inherently unique to its individual participants.

One-to-one marketing has only recently become practical and cost-efficient on a large scale, because of what the computer now makes possible. Database technology allows an enterprise to track its customers individually and tell them apart. Interactive technologies, including

Web sites, call centers and sales force automation tools, provide an automated connection from the customer to the firm, enabling a company to receive feedback, including product and service specifications, from its individual customers. And mass customization technology permits a firm to configure its offering digitally, in effect mass-producing a product in lot sizes of one.

So, rather than sampling a "market" of potential customers to determine what the average customer in the market needs, the 1to1 marketer focuses on one customer at a time. Using these three types of computer technology—the database, interactivity and mass customization—the marketer can set up a relationship that goes like this:

"I know you, you're in my database. You tell me what you want, and then I'll make it for you that way."

This interaction is then likely to become part of an ongoing series of linked interactions, together building a richer context for the relationship over time.

"Last time we did it this way. Would you like it more like this now? How about this? Is this better?"

With each interaction and recustomization—each time the firm and the customer re-engage in their relationship—the company is able to fit its product or service a little more closely to the needs of *that* customer. In effect, the relationship is getting smarter and smarter, becoming better and better at satisfying that particular customer's need. We call this type of relationship a "Learning Relationship."

When a customer is engaged in a Learning Relationship, it soon becomes more convenient for the customer simply to continue buying from the enterprise (even at an undiscounted price) than it would be for her to reteach the firm's competitor what she wants.

Two examples that spring to mind are Amazon.com and British Airways. Amazon not only recognizes you as a returning customer whenever you visit but, with your permission, it "remembers" your reading preferences, your credit card numbers and your shipping addresses. When you fly British Airways, the flight attendants will access your profile from the customer database to help them "remember," on behalf of the airline, the amenities you prefer.

The contrast between 1to1 marketing and traditional marketing is interesting. While the key metric of success for a traditional marketer is market share, measured one product category at a time, the success metric for a 1to1 marketer is share of customer, measured one customer at a time. A traditional marketer tries to find more customers for her products, but a 1to1 marketer tries to find more products and services for her customers. A traditional marketing company manages products, holding its executives accountable for quarterly sales of these products, while a 1to1 marketer manages customers, holding its executives accountable for growing the expected values of these customers, over time.

Obviously, the organizational issues that surround this are important. Traditional marketing can be done in a "silo" department, more or less independently of other, nonmarketing functions at a firm. Hire a marketing director, run an advertising or promotional campaign, and then sell the products through the standard retail outlets, or whatever other distribution channels are being used.

But 1to1 marketing involves tracking an individual customer's patronage over time, managing a continuing series of interactions with the customer, and measuring the customer's business across different products or groups of products and services. Needless to say, these activities require a high degree of integration. Not only do they pose a significant threat to any existing distribution channel, but just managing a serious one-to-one marketing effort can mean rethinking the organizational structure, the information systems, and the budgeting and reward structure within the firm. It is because the nature of 1to1 marketing is so integrative that it can be problematic to label it "marketing" at all. The process will, of necessity, involve the entire enterprise in an effort to treat each different customer as individually as possible across every function, department and division at the enterprise. That's why we say that, for a firm to get serious about 1to1 marketing, it must turn itself into a 1to1 enterprise.

Despite these obstacles, one-to-one marketing is an idea whose time has come. According to a recent survey of 200 senior executives around the world, by the year 2002 roughly 50 percent of companies are likely to be organized around customer type, compared to 18 percent today. And more than 60 percent of the businesses represented in this survey cited "changing customer demographics and needs" and the "pressure to customize" their offerings in light of these changes, as the most profound influences on their current business strategies.

The process of implementing a one-to-one marketing program, or a CRM initiative, can be thought of as a series of four basic steps: *identify, differentiate, interact* and *customize*. These steps are roughly in order of increasing difficulty and complexity, even though you may find a good deal of overlap among them:

1. *Identify* your customers. You can't have a relationship with someone you can't identify, so it's absolutely critical to "know" customers individually, in as much detail as possible, and to be able to recognize them across all contact points, through all media, across every product line, at every location, and in every division. If a company hasn't acquired the addressable identities of at least a fair number of its most valuable customers, then it isn't yet prepared to launch a one-to-one initiative. (Or perhaps it hasn't defined its customers the right way, and should be trying to create relationships with intermediaries and channel members, rather than with end-users.) For a retailer, for instance, the process of identifying customers might involve some type of frequent buyer program, designed to give a customer an incentive to "hold up his hand" every time he comes into the store. For a business-to-business firm, on the other hand, the identification step might involve trying to learn the specific names and positions of those executives, within a customer's organization, who have an influence on the buying decision.

2. *Differentiate* your customers. Customers are different in two principal ways: They represent different levels of value to you (some are very valuable, some not so

valuable), and they have different needs. So, once you identify your customers, the next step is to differentiate them so as to (a) prioritize your efforts and gain the most advantage with the most valuable customers, and (b) tailor your firm's behavior toward each customer based on that customer's individual needs. Obviously, this implies that the business will develop some type of ranking criteria, or customer profitability and valuation model. But it also means that the firm must begin categorizing customers by their differing needs, to prepare to treat different customers differently.

3. *Interact* with your customers. To implement a one-to-one program, you must improve both the cost efficiency and the effectiveness of your interactions with customers. That is, not only do you want interactions that are less expensive and possibly more automated, but you want them to be more useful, in terms of producing information that can help you strengthen and deepen your customer relationships. Also, every interaction with a customer should take place in the context of all previous interactions *with that customer*. A conversation should pick up where the last one left off, whether the previous interaction occurred last night or last month, at the call center, on the company Web site, or in the customer's own office while meeting with the company's salesperson. The interaction step is involved intimately with both the differentiation step and the customization step. In addition to knowing how your customers' needs vary, you must have a methodology for using the interactive feedback

from a particular customer to deduce *that* customer's particular needs. Then, based on that information, you embark on the next implementation step.

4. *Customize* some aspect of your enterprise's behavior toward your customer. To lock a customer into a Learning Relationship, a firm must adapt some aspect of its behavior to meet that customer's individually expressed needs. This might mean mass customizing a manufactured product, or it could involve tailoring some aspect of the services surrounding a product. To practice true 1to1 marketing, the production or service delivery end of your business must be able to treat a particular customer differently based on what *that customer* said during an interaction with the sales or marketing part of your firm. A common misconception about 1to1 marketing is that, because it stretches down to the granular level of every single customer, every single customer must receive a uniquely different offer or message. That is a worthy goal, but what 1to1 marketing really means is simply treating different customers differently, in a way that is meaningful to the individual customers. This sort of tailoring can only be done cost efficiently by using a mass customization methodology—creating a variety of highly specific products out of pre-existing components, or modules. Twelve A modules, when combined with 25 B modules, 16 C modules and 13 D modules, are enough to generate more than 60,000 possible products. Note that only 66 modules are actually involved in configuring this vast assortment of different products. That's

how mass customization works. Moreover, applying this process to the way you treat a customer is not just about physical product attributes. You can mass-customize the way products or services are packaged, configured, delivered, invoiced, arranged, financed or reported. You can mass-customize the way calls are handled at a call center, and the way visitors are treated at a Web site.

Applied in different ways, these four simple implementation steps—identify, differentiate, interact and customize—can be used as a checklist for putting into practice virtually any CRM initiative, at virtually any firm, facing any kind of business situation. To make incremental progress toward becoming a better relationship marketer, most firms begin simply by implementing projects that can be categorized as belonging to one or more of these four steps.

Over and above the actual implementation steps, however, the process of becoming a true 1to1 enterprise will almost certainly require a firm to rethink its most basic business philosophies, overhaul the attitudes of its managers and employees, and probably even reconstruct its very culture. There is more involved here than simply putting a great e-commerce Web site into effect, or launching a call center, or automating the sales force. Doing business as a 1to1 enterprise means viewing the entire business from the customer's perspective.

So Old It Seems New

Treating different customers differently is an old concept, dating back to the very beginnings of trade and commerce. We began to lose sight of this concept amid the excesses of the Industrial Revolution and the decades of global turmoil that followed. The astonishing success of mass production as a means for adequately feeding, clothing and equipping unprecedented numbers of people pushed the concept even further into the background. Now, in a moment of global peace and prosperity, we finally have the chance to take a breath, look around at the world we've created and ask ourselves, "How can we make this better?" There are many answers. One of those answers is returning the focus of business to the individual relationships between buyers and sellers. If we've learned anything from the last two hundred years, it's that the individual *does* matter.

ONCE UPON A TIME . . .

Hundreds of years ago, bankers would transact business with their customers while seated on benches in the marketplace. Those benches, or "banquettes," gave the industry its name. The bankers knew their individual customers by name and knew their financial needs. The use of money and credit was not widespread, so the pool of potential customers was relatively small. Nonetheless, the bankers reaped handsome profits because they intuitively grasped a fundamental rule of one-to-one marketing: *Each customer has different needs and brings different value to the relationship.* Not every prince was an excellent credit risk and not every troubadour was a deadbeat.

Let's follow several generations of a "typical" family to see how they do business with their bankers. Our story begins in 1850 with Jacques Roberts, a sailmaker in New Bedford, Massachusetts. His customers are the owners and captains of the whaling vessels that sail from New Bedford to all watery points of the globe. Each time a ship returns to port, it needs a complement of new sails to replace those that were torn and tattered during the voyage. Jacques knows the schedule of each ship and what kind of sails each carries. He makes sure he has enough canvas to cut and sew into mainsheets, foresails, mizzen topsails, topgallant staysails, flying jibs and spankers. Sometimes, however, he's caught short. If an unexpected gale or nor'easter pummels the coast, the demand for replacement sails might be especially high.

When that happens, Jacques needs to raise cash to buy canvas—and fast. So he walks over to the Salt and Spray Bank of New Bedford, sits down with the bank's owner and explains his needs. The banker has known Jacques for years. Their families attend the same church, belong to the same clubs and share similar dreams for the future. The banker is aware that Jacques plays an important role in keeping the local economy healthy—because if the ships don't have sails, they can't leave port. And if the ships don't leave port, they don't bring back the whale oil that fuels the New England economy. And if the New England economy falters, the growing national economy suffers.

The banker doesn't hesitate to open a line of credit for Jacques so he can buy all the canvas he needs. Jacques makes the sails, the ships sail away and everyone touched by the process prospers—because Jacques and his banker have a one-to-one relationship.

Let's skip ahead to 1920 and visit with Jacques's grandson Jack, who is a farmer in Olathe, Kansas. A long drought has made it hard for Jack to accumulate the cash he needs to buy seed for the next planting. So Jack drives his Model T over to the Earth and Loam Bank of Olathe, sits down with the bank president, and explains his situation. The bank president listens carefully. He knows exactly how much Jack is worth because the bank manages Jack's savings account, wrote the mortgage on Jack's farm and holds the paper on several loans Jack secured to purchase new farm equipment. The banker also knows the value of Jack's property (as collateral) and the potential value of his next crop, which will determine his ability to pay off the loan. After factoring in Jack's reputation for hard work and resourcefulness, the banker arranges short-term financing and Jack heads off to the general store to buy seed. Because he has an ongoing one-to-one relationship with Jack, the banker is comfortable making the loan. Jack's needs are served and the banker's needs are served.

WHY DON'T THEY KNOW ME?
Now shift focus to the present. Jack's grandson Jake is the CEO of a small company in San Diego that makes custom sails for racing yachts. Jake does most of his banking

at Consolidated Aggregate Bank of North America, which maintains a branch near the marina. Consolidated Aggregate handles Jake's personal savings and checking accounts, issues his credit cards, holds his mortgage, wrote his car loan and manages his IRAs. The bank also handles Jake's business needs, arranging loans and credit lines. The bank even arranged the financing for Jake's leased corporate car. If the bank were a one-to-one marketer, it would consider Jake a Most Valuable Customer and would strive to treat him differently from its less valuable customers.

But when Jake goes to the bank to make a deposit, he stands in the same line as everyone else. When he fills out an application to refinance his mortgage, not only does he have to start with the same blank form as everyone else— he has to send it to another branch to be processed. If he misses a payment on his credit card, he's charged a stiff penalty and his card privileges are temporarily suspended. When he asks the bank about starting a special investment fund for his daughter's postgraduate education, he is given a form and told to fill in his name, his address, his Social Security number and dozens of other items of personal data the bank already has on file. "Why don't they know me?" wonders Jake. "I've been doing business with them forever!"

So it's not surprising that, when Jake gets an offer in the mail from a national bank offering a lower credit card rate, he takes it. And when the Monumental Amalgamated Bank down the block offers no-minimum free checking for life, Jake closes his account at Consolidated

Aggregate and opens a new one at Monumental Amalgamated. When Monumental runs an ad for low-interest mortgage refinancing with no points, Jake refinances. Over several months, Jake transfers more than $500,000 worth of business from Consolidated to Monumental—and neither bank seems to notice! It won't be long before Jake moves his business to yet another bank, and then another.

It's easy to see that Jake doesn't have the kind of intimate relationship with his bankers that his ancestors enjoyed. How did this breakdown occur? Simply put, the economies of scale and mass production made it easier for many industries to become product-focused instead of customer-focused. Banks also followed this trend, creating separate product lines for home loans, car loans, credit cards, savings, checking etc. This compartmentalization, however, has made it all but impossible to measure the potential value of an individual customer across the width and breadth of the corporation.

Now consider that each of these separate product lines is likely to have its own information system, which means that vital customer information is spread haphazardly throughout the enterprise instead of stored centrally. And remember that new data continuously enter these various systems though several points of contact including tellers, branch managers, loan officers, ATMs, call centers and the Internet.

Certainly, the challenges are daunting. But looking ahead, it's easy to predict the demise of business practices that discourage, rather than encourage, customer loyalty.

In the very near future it will be considered highly unusual for a bank—or any business, for that matter—to be unable or unwilling to track individual customers across various portfolios or product lines.

FAST-FORWARD TO THE OLD DAYS

It's safe to say that Jake's daughter Jackie will have a very different experience when she "visits" her bank in 2020. Jackie Roberts has decided to follow in the footsteps of her great-grandfather, Jack. She's an organic farmer in Terre Haute, Indiana, and a loyal customer of Central Agro Banc—a bank that exists mostly in cyberspace. As far as Jackie is concerned, the bank is wherever she is—all she has to do is turn to her personal digital device, which is continuously logged on to the network. The "bank" knows Jackie immediately, and displays a unique collection of icons accurately reflecting her various accounts, available credit, purchasing history, personal preferences and status as a customer.

If the bank has a promotional message for Jackie, it will be chosen specifically for her. For instance, perhaps she decides to check her credit to explore how much of a car she could afford to lease. The bank might suggest an auto insurance upgrade and a roadside assistance plan, which isn't covered in some leases. Some of her lease can be written off as a tax deduction, so the bank shows her the tax savings she will realize after deducting different percentages of the lease.

More important, she won't have to identify herself over and over again—all the information about her will be instantaneously and easily accessible. If, for example, she wants to apply for a new mortgage, she won't have to fill out a five-page application. When she needs a corporate credit card, she won't have to approach the bank as if she were a new customer—because the entire bank's business lines will be fully integrated. From the moment of Jackie's first encounter with the bank she will be treated as an individual customer with unique and special needs. If Jackie decides actually to visit a branch of her bank in person, her experience won't be too much different from the experiences of her great-grandparents. That's because the one-to-one bank would know the needs and value of each customer—the same way that bankers of the past knew the needs and value of their individual customers.

In the ideal one-to-one bank, every customer's value will be calculated from an enterprise-wide perspective, rather than from the perspective of an individual product line. Sales, marketing and service processes will be automated. Customer information will flow seamlessly across the enterprise, accessible to any and all who need it. Managers will be able to drill down into a large, reliable, unified database to study customer activity by geography, demography, revenue, market segment and a variety of other variables. The tellers, the branch managers, the sales force, the call center operators—everyone at the bank who has contact with customers—will be fully trained and properly equipped to take maximum advantage of the bank's integrated, synchronized information technologies. Each customer will be tracked through every stage of his or her relationship with the bank, yielding up a treasure trove of valuable data. In such an environment, previously unseen connections and underlying relationships will rise into view, offering opportunities to dramatically increase customer retention, cross sell, up sell and enhance profitability.

Pre-Existing Circumstances

The process of transforming your company into a 1to1 enterprise is complex and difficult. The discussions that follow will make it abundantly clear that anyone who gets involved in a 1to1 marketing program should be prepared for setbacks, unanticipated problems and a certain amount of internal resistance. That being said, you can optimize your chances for success by taking it one step at a time.

One of the reasons the vast expanse of North America proved relatively easy to explore and settle in such a brief period of time was the presence of large navigable rivers such as the Ohio, the Missouri, the Arkansas and the Colorado, which allowed east/west travel across the continent. Compare this with Russia, where major rivers such as the Dnieper, the Don, the Volga and the Lena tend to run north/south, hampering transcontinental communication and travel. Luck and pre-existing circumstance play significant roles in determining final outcomes. The playing field isn't always level. While all companies will eventually face a choice of either embracing customer relationship management concepts or going out of business, it's also fair to say that some industries are more naturally suited to a one-to-one environment than others.

A recent conversation we had with Steve Wiggins underscored this observation. An early believer in one-to-one theory, Wiggins learned the hard way that successful customer initiatives can mutate swiftly into disasters if they are allowed to spin out of control—which is what happened at Oxford Health Plans.

With the clarity of vision afforded only by hindsight, Wiggins now believes that companies with highly complex products or those requiring heavy human-to-human customer contact are not ideal *early* candidates for one-to-one initiatives. The managed care industry, with its infinite range of unpredictable outcomes and frequent need for human intervention, has proved extraordinarily difficult to pin down. Nowhere has this been demonstrated more starkly than at Oxford.

Perhaps the most important lesson to draw from Oxford's travails, however, is that it's impossible to resist an idea whose time has arrived. Despite a series of highly publicized setbacks, the company has lost only a handful of customers and continues to sign up new ones—a testament to the enduring strength of carefully nurtured customer relationships.

Companies with large numbers of data points *can* be promising candidates for 1to1 programs if customer interactions can be automated to some degree. Financial products, for example, lend themselves especially well to one-to-one processes. First, they are by nature easy to define—even the most complicated trading scenarios involve little more than buying, selling and keeping track of accounts. Financial service companies such as USAA, First Union and First USA Bank have implemented innovative one-to-one strategies to ascertain the value of individual customers and to treat different customers differently—all with a resounding, positive impact on the bottom line. This leads to an entirely different way to view the situation: If this is such a compelling idea, why aren't *all* financial institutions implementing it today? Stay tuned.

We have found that a thoughtfully planned, incremental approach is almost always the best. Keep an eye out for quick, easy victories. Embracing the 1to1 philosophy will necessarily involve changing a company's culture, and changing the culture is a long and difficult process. You'll notice that few of our 1to1 managers have made a clean break with the past. This is perfectly natural. In fact, we believe it's unlikely that "traditional" mass marketing tactics will ever vanish completely. What we can say with some certainty, however, is that companies that fail to develop viable 1to1 strategies will find themselves facing a distinct competitive disadvantage as commerce continues to evolve from "product-centric" to "customer-centric."

If there is a paramount virtue shared by our one-to-one managers, that virtue is patience. The universal words of caution are these: "Don't try to do it all at once." And don't lose sight of the fact that you've embarked on a revolutionary path. Not everyone is going to have the capacity or the desire to follow you right away. Do try to get as much understanding and agreement within your firm as possible before you begin. Don't shoot for the stars on the first day. Set reasonable goals and don't raise expectations beyond your capability to deliver. Have confidence, stay the course and you'll succeed. Luckily, the tide is with you.

1

Trusted Agents

Why is this simple term—*trusted agent*—so loaded with meaning? Because, as a company tries to strike up one-to-one relationships with its individual customers, it soon realizes that the single most powerful position in any customer's mind is a position of trust. For that reason, earning the customer's trust almost always becomes one of the earliest goals in any effort to build a long-term relationship with a customer.

Only in a relationship of trust can information pass back and forth freely between buyer and seller. And, in a world of increasingly commodity-like products and services, a relationship founded on trust is the only genuinely sustainable competitive edge. Without trust, you're back to square one—competing on price.

Trust is the currency of all commerce.

Take a moment to consider the Internet. Suddenly you have the capability to network your intelligence with the intelligence of every other human being on the planet with access to a PC and a modem. As the novelty of this phenomenon wears off, the reality will set in: The only networking you'll really want to do is with the people and organizations with which you already have some sort of relationship. And the more trusting that relationship is, the more likely it is that you will be willing to share and exchange your knowledge.

On the other side of this relationship—on the enterprise's side—becoming a trusted agent is usually not an easy thing to accomplish. A trusted agent is one that can be relied upon to make the customer's interests paramount, to speak on the customer's behalf in all its dealings. As a policy, this is a heretical undertaking at most companies, and flies in the face of product-centered principles of marketing and competition. If you and I have no relationship prior to the purchase, and we have no relationship following it, then our entire interaction is centered on a single, solitary transaction. And our interests are diametrically opposed. I want to buy the most product at the lowest price from you, and you want to sell me the least product at the highest price.

In a transaction-based, product-centric business model, buyer and seller are adversaries, no matter how much the seller may try not to act the part. In this kind of business model, practically the only assurance a customer has that she can trust the product and service being sold to her is the general reputation of the brand itself.

But in a 1to1 marketing model the purchase transaction exists within the context of previous transactions and more that will follow. Moreover, the buyer and seller collaborate, with the buyer interacting to specify the product, and the seller responding with some change in behavior appropriate for *that* buyer. In the CRM business model, in other words, the buyer and seller must be willing to trust each other far beyond the general reputation of the brand.

Translating a "trusted agent" philosophy into commercial reality involves more than simple policy decisions on the enterprise's part, no matter how revolutionary those policies might be. Becoming a trusted agent for your customer requires a deep, cultural change in attitude at most firms.

But at the most basic level, a genuinely trusted agent must be able to *remember* an individual customer from transaction to transaction, division to division, across the length and breadth of the enterprise. Customer relationships, in other words, *must be integrated into every aspect of the business process,* so as to harmonize products and services throughout the organization. Without integration, the left hand won't know what the right hand is doing.

It's easy to see that if one division sells aircraft engines and the other sells aircraft engine maintenance contracts, then it makes sense that they should work together— even if tradition dictates otherwise. But the same logic applies in a variety of other situations, some obvious and some not so obvious. One business unit might sell copiers while a sister unit sells toner cartridges and another sister unit sells copier paper. Or one division might sell postage meters while another sells automated mailroom services.

Or one sells home mortgages, while another sells credit cards, and yet another sells savings accounts.

Integrating the way an individual customer is treated throughout the enterprise is essential to creating a relationship with that customer and represents the very first, most basic step toward earning her trust. What integration amounts to, as a concept, is simply ensuring that the way the firm behaves toward a particular customer appears "rational" to her. Rationality is achieved when all parts of your enterprise coordinate their activities with respect to this particular customer, based on what she has told you about herself and her needs, and what other things you already know about her.

Such coordination is going to be costly and difficult. But to create a position as a trusted agent in the mind of your customer, you have to develop empathy for the customer. You have to coordinate your activities with respect to that customer, to be able to put yourself in the place of the customer, to take a customer view. And it might be expensive to put the necessary systems into place. But, as one UK consultant put it, if you think empathy is going to be expensive, then you should try apathy.

The central message being brought to you by the pioneers and visionaries in this book is not that creating relationships with customers is difficult and costly. We already know that. The message from these pioneers is that *failing* to create such relationships might actually prove to be fatal.

Company: First USA
(WILMINGTON, DELAWARE)

Pioneer: Richard Vague, CEO

Lesson: You don't win the race by being the best but by staying the best. If you have a great customer acquisition engine, then the next step should be to invent a great customer retention engine.

Richard Vague didn't learn much about customer relationships on his first job. He was a busboy at Denny's in Houston. You can't really fault him for not paying more attention to the people who came into the restaurant to gobble down a quick meal, since his main objective was to avoid breaking dishes on the way back to the kitchen. If your job involves carrying heavy loads of food-encrusted plates, bowls, cups, saucers and silverware all day long, one of the first things you learn is to avoid distractions, and in that context customers are a distraction. Vague's next job, however, was working behind the counter at a local dry cleaner. That's where his perspective on customers began to change. "I really got to like them and prided myself on knowing their names. I got to know them so well that I could have their cleaning out and ready for them before they made it through the front door."

Vague hadn't planned on becoming a banker. But when he was twenty and putting himself through college, he ran out of money and had to find work. A local bank hired him as an account analysis clerk. "I've stayed in the business ever since," he says, smiling. These days, however, Vague earns his daily bread as chairman and CEO of First USA, the nation's largest and most innovative issuer of Visa, MasterCard and private label credit cards. But he relates the story of his dry cleaning days with a boyish enthusiasm that remains undimmed by the passage of years. Listening to Vague makes it easier to understand why First USA launched *At Your Request,* a remarkably ambitious service program that "acts as your personal assistant, concierge, researcher and travel agent, all in one."

Melding his personal experiences with a growing belief in the idea of 1to1 marketing, Vague envisioned First USA developing highly personalized relationships with its customers. He wants his bank to become a "trusted agent" for customers, in the process generating an involvement on each customer's part that would make it hard to simply walk away when other cards beckon with lower APRs, as they always will.

At Your Request works like this: After you've been a credit card customer in good standing for at least a year, First USA sends you an invitation to sign up for the service. You fill out a Preference Profile that asks for the names and birthdays of everyone in your immediate family. You are also asked to specify hobbies, favorite magazines, sports and cultural pursuits. *At Your Request* includes a reminder service called *Just-in-Time.* You are asked to list anniversaries, special events and important dates, such as an appointment with your doctor or your car's next oil change. Finally you are asked when and how you'd like to be notified of an upcoming event—you can choose between e-mail or fax.

At Your Request customers can contact the service via

telephone, e-mail or the World Wide Web. Staffed by about 50 advisers and researchers, the service offers three broad areas of help—financial, travel/entertainment and general information/gift/reminder. "We help people locate everything from antique telescopes to flintlock rifles. If you need a reservation at a restaurant or you need to send flowers, we can do that for you. One time we got a call from a customer who was getting married in Switzerland and needed a rabbi. We found one. Another time we had a customer who was living next door to a house that had been condemned and was going to ruin. We were able to get the house sold at a sheriff's auction. Now it's all fixed up and our customer's property is worth a whole lot more. Basically, we'll try to do anything we can to help you."

Customers are required to use their First USA credit cards if the inquiry results in a purchase. Fewer than half of the calls to *At Your Request,* however, result in a purchase. Most are purely requests for information. "For example, if you're relocating and need information about your new neighborhood, we'll send you a list of schools or whatever you need to feel comfortable." In a sense, says Vague, *At Your Request* is a search engine that's custom-built around the needs of First USA's customers. "You couldn't dream of doing this if it weren't for the Internet, which has dramatically lowered the cost of obtaining information. I'd say the cost of information—if it isn't approaching zero—is a lot closer to zero than it ever was before."

Vague says the return on *At Your Request* can't be measured exclusively in terms of credit card activity. "It occurred to us that playing the role of concierge would do two things. First of all, it would augment our knowledge of the customer. If somebody calls up and says, 'What's the best deal on a kayak?' that tells us a lot about him. If someone calls to plan a vacation with her family, we will learn—while answering her questions—valuable information about that family. If we know, for example, there is a ten-year-old in the family, when that child turns fifteen and a half we're going to send the parents information about the best deals on new driver insurance. Second, our being genuinely helpful would create a feeling of trust in the customer's mind. So the customer wouldn't just see us as a big institution coming at them to sell something. We found when we *did* occasionally market something to them, such as a new financial planning service matched to their needs, we got a significantly higher response rate—which is pretty amazing. In our business, a 1 percent response rate is considered huge."

If Vague has his way, the response rate will climb far higher. In his mind, the separation between credit card issuers and "the spending habits of consumers" is purely artificial, an arbitrary barrier that inhibits lenders and consumers from working together. "Over the long haul, the only game is to become a trusted agent of the customer," says Vague.

ACTIVE ROLE

Balancing the company's own, commercial interests against the need to provide objective, impartial advice to customers was another issue that First USA wrestled with when implementing the *At Your Request* service. The economics of the program depend partly on commissions from vendors. If a customer books a trip to Hawaii through *At Your Request,* for instance, First USA will earn a commission on the air tickets and hotel stay. And this applies to merchandise sales, too. First USA has made arrangements with a number of vendors to ensure that when its customers are recommended to them, the bank receives a commission on the sale.

But suppose a customer requests information on, say, the best CD player for her living room. Should First USA only show her CD players from companies with whom it has made a sales arrangement? It's clearly in the bank's interest to promote those deals, but what's the right way to balance this commercial interest against the bank's other objective—serving as a trusted agent for its customers' own best interests?

The solution First USA arrived at is actually pretty simple. When a customer makes a request for such information, the service lists for her a variety of products, referencing some impartial third party whenever possible—perhaps *Consumer Reports,* or maybe a different magazine. For example, "These are the top five CD players, according to . . ." Underneath this listing, however, the bank also shows the particular CD players manufactured by companies with which it has made sales arrangements, and offers the customer a special deal if she chooses to buy one of these products.

Clearly, in order for Vague to push his bank's role as a trusted agent his company must take an active role in helping customers satisfy their varied needs. So, First USA developed a proprietary software system that enables it to extract a wider range of data from each credit card transaction. Gathering genuinely useful data from MasterCard and Visa transactions has always been difficult, but First USA is heading toward solving the problem. With the transactional data in hand, First USA uses it to create a highly accurate, rank-ordered description of an individual customer's actual preferences. The data are displayed as an indexed ratio of spending, so various categories of purchases can be compared reliably and consistently.

"Essentially, you're voting with your credit card on what is most and least interesting to you," Vague says. "Soon we'll have a system that has so much data that we'll be able to look at the aggregate and determine by sheer weight of numbers the spending preferences across our whole customer base. Then I can take one of those preferences to a merchant, get the best deal ever and start offering that deal to my customers. And the really great thing is that it's a perpetually refreshing loop, because new purchase information is coming in every day. And we've built the system to selectively forget some things. For example, if you bought a new set of golf clubs, we would 'remember' that information for quite a while, because you're not likely to buy another set of clubs for another four or five years. If you've bought toys for your kids, it only makes sense for us to 'remember' that information for a year or so."

In a very real way, Vague is allowing the aggregate individualized behavior of the bank's customer base to drive marketing decisions. Instead of relying solely on top-down, management-driven policies and strategies,

First USA is placing its trust in closely monitored "customer-created" programs to go where no modern bank has gone before—right back to the ancient beginnings, when banks existed to serve their customers.

"Technology, which has been accused of impersonalizing relationships over the last thirty or forty years, is now returning us to a point where interactions with our customers are highly personalized," says Vague. Technology-enabled programs such as *At Your Request* help the company assemble an accurate and up-to-date picture of an individual customer's real and perceived needs. Credit bureau information, financial data provided by the customer and the bank's own highly detailed records of credit card transactions allow First USA to calculate an individual customer's potential value to the bank with uncanny precision. First USA calculates both the actual and projected profitability of its customer base quarterly, enabling it to stay on course as it moves ahead to achieve the one-to-one vision. Access to this wide range of up-to-date information empowers the bank to view its customers as long-term partners engaged in a continuously unfolding series of mutually beneficial relationships.

"It's very much a trailblazing activity," says Vague, mindful of the danger, but thrilled to play the role of a technology-empowered explorer. "Although we're the biggest in the industry, we are still always looking for an edge—some way of doing something different or better for the customer."

Reflecting on the past, Vague notes that one of his boyhood heroes was Miles Davis, the magically talented and mercurial jazz trumpeter. "He was very innovative.

But he also hired very, very strong players to be in his band, guys who were as good or better than he was. That's important if you're going to succeed."

Company: Franklin University
(COLUMBUS, OHIO)

Pioneer: Dr. Paul Otte, president

Lesson: When you implement a system of customer management, it's important to ensure that the customers see the managers as being on their *side. You want to be the trusted agent of your customer.*

Other than buying your dream house, paying for a big wedding, or getting that sweet car you can't really afford, there's no other more costly, once-in-a-lifetime purchase for most people than a college education. And there's probably no process that will leave a consumer more frustrated and less satisfied than the logistics of getting that degree. Consider this brief list of all-too-familiar scenarios:

- Labyrinthine lines that lead to someone as uninformed as you are.
- Documents that, like a scavenger hunt, send you all over the campus to get the right signatures.
- Advisers who are never in their offices.
- Bursars who smile (a little) only when the tuition check is handed over.

Satisfaction guaranteed? Not likely. The typical college business model views students as *product*. Like widgets. Students arrive as raw material, they are processed by faculty and emerge as graduates, ready for additional processing at a postgraduate facility.

If this imagery is frightening, join us for a visit to a one-to-one campus. At Franklin University in Columbus, Ohio, named after the innovative and consumer-friendly inventor, Benjamin Franklin, the students are viewed as customers. As Franklin University President Dr. Paul Otte is fond of saying: "The customer is not always right, but the customer is always the customer." Even when the customer is a student.

Franklin University is an independent, nonprofit, metropolitan facility that is home to eighteen undergraduate and three graduate programs. The school is recognized as one of the top specialty business institutions in the nation and serves more than 5,000 students annually—90 percent of whom hold full- or part-time jobs. Otte says the university's greatest success is taking "dissatisfied customers from other educational experiences and turning them into satisfied customers." In fact, Otte says, 85 percent of the university's new students transfer from other colleges "with horror stories that are amazing."

What makes Franklin unique, says Otte, is that it applies 1to1 principles aggressively to manage its relationships with students. Franklin eliminates many of the frustrating barriers to achieving educational goals by providing easily accessible support through its Student Services Associate program. Each student is assigned an

SSA, who essentially guides them through every step of the educational process, right up to graduation. "We try to make everything other than going to class transparent to the students, all the way from giving them a parking sticker when they walk in, to how they register," Otte says.

Students are matched with an SSA based on their academic major and any additional circumstances worth taking into account. International students, for example, are assigned SSAs who are familiar with the issues likely to confront a foreign national living in the United States. Disabled students are paired with SSAs who understand the special obstacles they routinely face.

The SSA's job is to

- help students clarify their educational and career goals;
- assist in the periodic review of academic progress;
- assist in preparing a chronological degree plan;
- perform "degree audits" to specify remaining academic requirements for degree completion;
- assist in scheduling classes; and
- serve as a liaison between the student and other university departments.

"We start with the assumption that the person walking in the door to our institution has the following standard profile: He or she has come from another institution, has college credit and, to a large degree, a chip on the shoulder," says Otte. "They're not bad students; they didn't leave for academic reasons for the most part. In fact, if we look at their composite profile, they have higher GPAs than the average. But a lot of them have chips on their shoulders. What we tell our SSAs is, 'You didn't put that chip there, but your job is to take it off. You need to own the chip, even though you didn't put it there.'"

The student-centered approach helps undergraduate and graduate students move quickly and easily through enrollment and registration so they can concentrate on other commitments, says Otte. Keenly aware that for working students time is precious, the university re-engineered and streamlined its various enrollment processes to the point where it takes a new student only one hour to apply, enroll and register. Even the school's new student services center was designed to minimize hassles for the student. In the past, students lined up at a counter to be served. "While we were in that industrial model, we were very efficient and we were faster than anyone else. You could still come in and register in an hour, but the person you saw last week might not be the person you see next week. The students never could develop a relationship."

Otte says that after rethinking the design—and reading *The Marketing Imagination* by Theodore Levitt—the counter was knocked down and a new reception area designed to make the facility more student-friendly. "We looked at it like a retailer would and we said, 'If we were a department store, we'd put our hot product in the number one location for sales.' The number one place here is the reception area for your SSA."

All of this special attention and handholding creates an unusually strong bond between the student and the SSA, Otte says. He likens it to a nurturing family relationship.

Sort of like having a big brother or big sister watching over you.

The decision to create a one-to-one university was dictated less by warm fuzzy feelings than by hard circumstances. Without something to differentiate it from the competition, Franklin was in danger of losing its reason for being. "We could have been out of business," Otte says. "Instead, with this program we went from a school where 60 percent of our students were freshmen and sophomores to one where 60 percent are now juniors and seniors, and we now have another 10 or 12 percent in our graduate school program. We knew we had to be the institution of choice for the transfer student and, according to the numbers, now we are."

Obviously, the strategy is working, when measured by the types of students the university is now attracting. It is also working from a financial standpoint, in terms of the volume of credit hours Franklin is now selling. Franklin University recently experienced seven consecutive terms in which the number of credit hours increased in comparison to the same term in the prior year.

In the past, the only way to achieve these kinds of improved numbers would have been to ratchet up the marketing budget in hopes of attracting more and more new students. But Franklin was able to change this pattern, to increase the volume of credit hours by increasing its *share of student*. In other words, the same students are simply taking more courses.

How did Franklin manage this? By making it less of a "hassle" to schedule a course and participate at the university, Franklin has given its students the opportunity to squeeze more courses into the same amount of time. And as it turns out, because of an Ohio state aid program, freeing up a student's time to take just one more course can also create a significant incentive for the student to do so.

"If you look at a typical, nontraditional college any-where in the country," Otte says, "that student is going to give the institution up to two nights a week part time. And you can't really alter that too much. So, if you went to most schools across the country that serve a population such as ours, the average credit hours they're carrying for their entire student body hovers around two courses. By doing more for the student, making courses available on an accelerated basis, making Saturday courses available, our SSAs are able to get students to take a third course. Now, we have a really neat advantage here, because when you take a third course, you're defined as a full-time stu-dent and the Ohio Choice Grant program kicks in. So you're actually getting two-thirds of the third course paid for by the state."

By any measure, the SSAs would be considered de-voted employees of the university. But their actual loyal-ties lie elsewhere. "Our Student Service Associates are loyal to the customer. They're not loyal to Franklin Uni-versity. We don't want them loyal to Franklin Univer-sity," Otte says. "Every day in our business the Student Service Associate makes decisions that cost us money. . . . I'm saying that satisfying the student will make Franklin University successful. When I teach a class, I'll say to the students a lot of the time—because I teach leadership and we use the SSA as an example—'Does that SSA make good financial decisions for Franklin each time you talk to them? No. And is that SSA loyal to the university or to you?' And they will say , 'To me. That SSA is working for me.' "

The SSA is another example of the trusted agent concept. The SSA is loyal to the student. The satisfied student is loyal to the university. Loyalty translates into retention. In general, retention leads to improved margins—because it's far less expensive to keep a good customer than to find a new one. In the case of the university, retention translates into higher revenues.

What happens if a student's SSA quits or becomes ill? "We profile our students on the computer," Otte says. "When a student calls and has a problem, whoever he's talking to can pull up the student's screen and see that profile. And if you're talking to a committed student, we're going to bend over backward for him. We may not take the same action for a student that's always putting excessive demands on the institution. In fact, we have said to some students, 'We really would like to give you your money back and suggest you go somewhere else because it's obvious we cannot meet your expectations.' "

There are twelve SSAs for the school's 5,000 students. An SSA remains with the same students through undergraduate and graduate school. That requires a very low turnover rate. How does Franklin University accomplish this feat? Otte says the answer is simple: Put the SSAs in the driver's seat. "In a typical college, these would be high-turnover jobs. Our retention of our SSAs has dramatically increased because each one, in effect, runs an institution of 500 students. They are making the calls.

Their partner in decision-making is the program chair of the major. As long as the two of them agree, it's a done deal."

In the end, everyone is happy because they're finally "treated like adults," Otte says. The students are allowed to concentrate on their studies. The SSAs become an integral, rather than tangential, part of the education process. In fact, they are evaluated on the basis of how many of their students make it to graduation. SSAs are required—*and paid*—to attend graduation ceremonies. They witness the results of their labor and share the excitement of the students and their families.

"Our graduations are the most serious, wonderful family events you have ever seen," says Otte. Most important, the students feel they are getting the most of their educational experience. In the words of one student: "My SSA does everything but go to the bookstore and buy books for me."

Thought Generator

At the end of each chapter, we raise an issue for discussion. We're calling these exercises "thought generators" because our goal is to go beyond the text and involve you more directly in the ongoing evolution of 1to1 marketing. At the end of each exercise you'll find a chapter-specific e-mail address. We invite you to share your thoughts, your insights, and your criticisms with us. We'll publish the best responses in our free weekly online newsletter, INSIDE 1to1. *As of this writing, each week's* INSIDE 1to1

*readership consists of nearly 200,000 CRM profes-
sionals around the world.*

Trusted Agents

The topic of customer retention is one of those
volatile areas in which logic, common sense, and
traditional wisdom seem to collide—often with
sad results.

Even though everyone agrees that it's far easier
and considerably less expensive to retain an existing customer than to find a new customer, most
companies still allocate the majority of their marketing dollars for customer acquisition, rather than
for customer retention. Many executives find it
difficult to overcome their prejudice against programs that don't result in acquiring more customers. Many still equate growth with increasing the
number, rather than the profitability, of customers.

So it's interesting to note that First USA's *At
Your Request* program—which requires extensive
resources to support—is not used for customer acquisition. Dick Vague is betting that by becoming
the trusted agent of his best customers, he will
achieve significantly higher retention rates and
that these higher retention rates will result in
greater profits.

Does your organization have similar customer
retention programs? If not, what's preventing you
from developing some?

We believe that it makes good business sense to strive toward the ideal of becoming your customer's trusted agent. Trust is the cornerstone of any lasting relationship. And, from a business standpoint, trust is relatively inexpensive. Why? Because you can begin to build trust by simply *not* doing some things, such as selling your mailing list or offering steep discounts to new customers. You can probably think of a dozen other ways in which your bond of trust with a customer could be broken or abused.

Here's the time for some genuine soul-searching. Do your company's policies and practices inspire trust or discourage it—especially among the customers you most want to keep and grow?

The next questions raise issues that many companies still prefer to ignore: Do you fairly compensate your employees for behaviors that inspire trust and support customer retention? Or are you rewarding your employees for merely *getting* more customers, no matter *who* they are? Who is clearly responsible for increasing *share of customer*, obtaining greater Lifetime Value and ensuring longer retention with an individual customer?

Consider this: If you were a bank, how would you compete with *At Your Request*?

Ask yourself if your firm could apply a version of Franklin University's Student Services Associate (SSA) program to manage its customer relationships. How would your organization measure the results of this type of customer management system?

Please e-mail your responses to
trustedagent@1to1.com

2

Using Technology

There is one very simple reason why more and more firms are beginning to practice 1to1 marketing: because they *can*. And the reason they can is that modern computer technology now makes it possible.

Three types of technology are necessary for an enterprise to be able to set up a long-term, continuously evolving Learning Relationship with a customer:

1. Databases, to provide a memory of the individual customer's transactions and interactions with the enterprise.
2. Interactive media, such as call centers, Web sites, an automated sales force or point-of-purchase automation, to allow customers to specify how they want to be treated.

3. Mass customization technology, or the digital configuration of products and services from preproduced modules, so that the enterprise can cost-efficiently treat its different customers differently.

Listening to customers and remembering what they say is the first half of the problem. The next step, however, is *acting* on the information obtained from a customer. This is the step that finally involves your customer and commits her to a Learning Relationship with your firm, making it more and more convenient for her to continue doing business with you, rather than taking the time and trouble to re-invent her relationship with one of your competitors.

The principles involved in 1to1 marketing may be as old as commerce itself. They certainly predate the principles of mass marketing. But mass production and mass marketing drove the cost of producing products and bringing them to market so low that relationships with individual customers were no longer practical. It is only since the invention of the microchip, and the information technologies the microchip has made possible, that modern companies can once again begin practicing the old art of customer relationship management, or 1to1 marketing.

Today, if you want to drive your own enterprise toward this type of competition, the surest, most productive course of action is to embrace information technology wholeheartedly. Keep the principles of 1to1 marketing firmly in mind, realize these principles will almost certainly involve changing the very nature of your business, and then implement them, using the latest, best, most capable information technology you can reasonably obtain.

Company: American Airlines
(FORT WORTH, TEXAS)

Pioneer: John Samuel, managing director of interactive marketing

Lesson: To use the Web the right *way you must mass-customize your site to meet the needs of your individual customers. Do it well, and this most sophisticated of interactive technologies can deliver the most sophisticated of personal service.*

John Samuel, managing director of interactive marketing at American Airlines, is the Cecil B. De Mille of Web-based relationship building. Indeed, if there were an Academy Award for the best online customer management program, a leading contender would be American Airlines. Its Web site (*www.AA.com*) has the capability to build custom pages on the fly, creating the potential for each of the airline's 2 million registered users—all members of American Airlines' "AAdvantage" frequent flyer program—to have a unique experience when visiting the site.

"This is the largest personalization effort on the Web," says Samuel. "And we believe we are still very much in the early stages." But as it is, AA.com offers an astounding level of personalization.

After logging on to the site's home page, members of American's frequent flyer program can create profiles based on home airport, preferred destination, preferred destination types (e.g., family, beach, golf, Europe), hub airports, hotel and rental car preferences, preferred class of service and seating preference. You can also store your credit card information, as well as the names of traveling companions and telephone numbers where you can be reached.

The next time you visit the site and log in, you will be greeted by name, and just under your name the total frequent flyer miles you have accumulated will be displayed. As you page through the site, you'll be shown customized news, information, special offers and travel packages, based on data from your profile and the records of your historical business with American. If you entered "golf" as one of your preferred destination types, for instance, your home page will automatically display the latest golf vacation packages, including any AAdvantage opportunities. If one of your preferred or regularly visited destinations is San Francisco, and that city is one of the destinations in the current week's offer, then a clickable Sale AAlert icon will be displayed on your personalized home page. When you click on the icon, you'll be shown fares and availability; simply clicking on the desired fare begins the booking process.

This site is so sophisticated, so personalized, that you might even be offered a special deal on vacation travel to the type of destination you prefer, during the week when *your* children are off from school in the school district where you live! And the site is fully transactional, so you can review or change an itinerary, price it, select and reserve a seat, and purchase the tickets with your credit card, all online.

Viewed from a strictly 1to1 perspective, AA.com is a testament to the wisdom of marrying basic, customer-focused sales and marketing techniques to currently available, high-technology resources. There are ancillary benefits, too. "Prior to the Web, there was no cost-effective way to tell millions of customers about a special fare available only this weekend," says Samuel. "Thanks to the interactive capability of the Web, we now can do exactly that." And without having to tell *everyone* about *every* special fare!

Implementing that Web capability was no small trick, however. American developed this personalized Web site (replacing an older site) using software from BroadVision Inc. of Palo Alto, California. The task was immensely complicated because, in order to do all the nifty things described above, the site had to be integrated into a whole series of other computer systems. The 36 million total AAdvantage members' records are tracked by an IBM DB2 mainframe database, a subset of which is copied daily to an Oracle database running on a Sun E4000 Web server to serve AA.com users. It is from the Oracle database that the Web site gets its AAdvantage member information, and as the member updates his file or changes his profile, this database is updated. Changes on either database are copied to the other to keep them in synch. When reservations need to be made, AA.com's booking application needs to be able to talk to a set of Digital VAX computer systems that run the Sabre reservations system on a VMS operating system.

One of BroadVision's strengths, as a product, is its open architecture, which lends itself to achieving this kind of back-end integration, which is not uncommon in large e-commerce applications. But the real strength of the BroadVision engine is that it applies mass customization principles to the Web. To render millions of different pages, and do it in a controlled, manageable way, a site must apply mass customization principles. BroadVision's process involves pre-specifying a number of templates and objects. These are the "modules" that can be combined to produce a wide variety of digitally configured "page views," based on the specific business rules that govern how the site is to be customized. (For example, "If a particular visitor has traveled to Europe more than two times in the last twelve months, then show the European companion-fare promotion.")

At the end of the day a marketing manager at American can get a complete picture of how the site is performing—what's hot and what's not—simply by reviewing tables of data that show the business rules triggered during the day. And any single customer's visit can be perfectly reconstructed by reviewing the business rules he triggered during his visit. Moreover, the manager can tweak the rules, altering the way the site customizes different offers for different visitors in real time, by accessing a special control center for the site, without having to write any code or take the system down. Millions of page combinations are possible at AA.com, but the entire site is managed through manipulating these business rules.

Most industry analysts now recognize BroadVision's One-to-One Web application as the most sophisticated, robust mass customization tool available. And one of the things it makes possible is the actual, rational *management* of the one-to-one marketing process—treating different customers differently, even when you have millions of them.

Company: Previnter
(BUENOS AIRES, ARGENTINA)

Pioneer: Gustavo Covacevich, CEO
Lesson: Technology doesn't need to be gold-plated to work. Look for simple ways to use technology to achieve your goals.

Gustavo Covacevich is *gerente general* of Previnter S.A., Argentina's fifth-largest private pension company. A joint venture of BankBoston and AIG, Previnter actively uses one-to-one strategies to combat an unbelievably high rate of customer turnover. Not long ago, Covacevich's sales manager told him that if he wanted his salespeople to be more productive, he should buy all 1,500 of them laptops. In his heart, Covacevich knew the issue with the sales force wasn't computing power. They needed something—a digital magic feather—to make the act of collecting customer information genuinely *important* to them.

And there was another issue: It had become too easy for sales reps to fake the activity reports they were required to file. These activity reports, which listed tele-phone calls and visits made to prospects, were considered an unnecessary annoyance by the sales staff. Covacevich was aware of this, but also believed it was essential to spur activity as a precursor to sales. "In reality, it's always eas-ier to measure actual sales than sales activity. I know that you can improve sales by improving activity, but how do you measure it? I had guys who were very good at selling, but when I asked them, 'How can we improve sales?' they'd say, 'Don't worry, we'll make our numbers.' Well, that wasn't good enough. I wanted more activity. Why? Because every call or visit contains a *moment of truth*—a special, unique moment that *must* be used to make the relationship grow."

So Covacevich reached into his jacket and whipped out the small electronic organizer he'd been using for years to keep track of telephone numbers and appoint-ments. "I didn't have the money to buy them all laptops," Covacevich recalls. "But I had some great people in our engineering department and I knew they could figure out a way to make these little $40 organizers do what we needed them to do. So I took this thing out of my pocket and said, 'Why can't we use this?' And my sales manager said, 'That's not what it was designed for,' and I said, 'Let's give it a try!' "

Today, when a sales rep from Previnter visits a client or prospect, he uses a specially modified, inexpensive pocket organizer to capture the significant details of the meeting. When the sales rep goes back to the office, he downloads the information into Previnter's central database, where it becomes available not only to his supervisors but to other sales reps as well. The immediate impact of the device, says Covacevich, was to increase sales activity dramatically—for the simple reason that the device generated a daily need for data that could not be faked. "Some people resigned," he says matter-of-factly. "But the people who stayed learned that this new tool actually made it easier to manage their client relationships. Activity increased and productivity increased."

Covacevich clearly loves telling this story. His idea to reconfigure an unsophisticated and unsexy device not only had a measurably positive effect on the company's sales force, but also helped sharpen Previnter's competitive edge by assuring a steady flow of timely, accurate customer information into the firm's central database. "I always try to find the link between marketing and technology," he says. "The challenge is to discover the right technology, grab it, adapt it to your needs and implement it. The process isn't all that complicated." The effort also yielded an unexpected bonus: Previnter now markets its homegrown pocket organizer modification as a product to other companies.

Company: Levi Strauss
(SAN FRANCISCO, CALIFORNIA)

Pioneer: *Gordon Shank, chief marketing officer*
Lesson: *Mass customization technology can have an impact far beyond the manufacturing process. It can change the entire marketing equation at a manufacturer, breathing new life into the very brand itself.*

In 1974, Gordon Shank drove his two-tone Chevrolet Monte Carlo across the plains of southern Ontario, his trunk full of dyed cotton garments. As Shank rode the highways of the Canadian province in that mud-splattered Chevy, the world around him was being transformed. The cultural revolutions of the 1960s had ousted mass conformity and replaced it with mass individuality. Shank had something in his trunk that appealed to the needs of an entire generation of nonconformists. As a result, he was a hero wherever he went. He was the Man with the Blue Jeans.

Shank worked for Levi Strauss & Co., the venerable San Francisco-based maker of reasonably priced, highly durable cotton clothing that had long been associated with the working class. In those days he would arrive at a store by 9 A.M., open his trunk, and pull out his sample merchandise. His selection: one style of blue denim pants (stone washed), two kinds of shirts (white and blue), and a blue denim jacket. For the truly adventurous there were corduroy trousers in three colors. "That's what we basically took to market," he recalls. "That was the total experience of Levi Strauss & Co. Canada, in 1974."

Levi Strauss & Co. had emerged from the sixties as the best-known maker of quintessential duds for people who saw themselves as hip—which, thanks to the influence of the mass media, seemed to be practically everyone. It was a generation of consumers that valued individuality, independence and self-expression above all other things. Levi's jeans were hot. Demand far exceeded supply. Throw a pair in the wash and they would shrink to fit. Take scissors to them and you could make your own shorts. The products weren't intentionally flashy or intrinsically sexy, but their simplicity fit a need. Levi's jeans became you.

By a happy accident of nature—cotton fiber shrinks when it's washed in hot water—Levi Strauss & Co. provided its customers with clothes that could be rendered unique. Customers could rip them, paint them, embroider them or sew a flag or peace symbol on them. Simple skills could transform them into something totally original. The clothing could be mixed and matched and tweaked and even tailored. Levi's jeans weren't customized, but they were customizable. It was a powerful competitive edge and the timing couldn't have been better. Over the next decade, however, Levi Strauss & Co. would learn that cotton wasn't always king and that it takes more than just "being there" to lock in customer loyalty.

But in 1974 being there was enough. Shank would go into a store and begin counting pairs of blue jeans on the shelves. Invariably, he had fewer blue jeans in his trunk than the storekeeper wanted. But what could the storekeeper do? As long as Shank could provide a steady stream of product, he had the upper hand. The view from corporate headquarters reinforced the notion that the product was invincible. "The prevailing belief was that brands controlled the dialogue. We make it, consumers come on down and buy it," recalls Shank. The very popularity of the product helped propel Shank and others of his generation up through the management ranks. Today he is chief marketing officer at the company, and while he remains extremely optimistic, his perspective has matured. "Twenty-five years ago there were far fewer players," Shank says with a sort of clear-eyed nostalgia. "The leaders were larger and had less competition."

Two things happened to change all this. The company's core customers grew older and more sophisticated. And suddenly, instead of facing just two major competitors (Lee and Wrangler), Levi Strauss & Co. now faced dozens, hundreds, maybe thousands around the world. As it turned out, the potential for self-customization wasn't enough to keep customers loyal—after all, you could do the same thing with other pairs of denims.

When serious competition surfaced, those end-user customers began to scatter. Even though Levi Strauss & Co. would eventually sell more than a million pairs of jeans a day around the world, it wasn't learning anything about why some end-users had left, because it had no way of collecting information about them or determining their individual needs. Consumers had no channel for communicating with the company, so they had no way of teaching Levi Strauss & Co. how to serve them better.

Overcoming challenges was nothing new to Levi Strauss & Co. The 145-year-old company had survived the destruction of its factory in the San Francisco earthquake of 1906. It had held on to customers even after the U.S. Government ordered design changes to conserve fabric during World War II. But the late 1970s and early 1980s—the Disco Era—forced a sea change on the apparel industry. Clothing-conscious consumers began seeking more urban, more cosmopolitan styles to satisfy their fashion needs. They began turning to high-profile designers such as Calvin Klein, Christian Dior, and Gloria Vanderbilt for blue jeans. Retailers that had been reliable wholesale customers unexpectedly emerged as direct competitors. J. C. Penney, for example, created its own private-label brand of jeans called "Plain Pockets."

By the mid-1980s, Levi Strauss & Co. knew it could no longer just go with the flow. Baby Boomers were still the bread and butter of its business, but they weren't buying as many blue jeans. One of the company's greatest successes of the 1980s—Dockers—became a billion-dollar business, but signaled more trouble just over the horizon. Yes, the Boomers were turning to cotton pants and Levi Strauss & Co. adroitly recognized this and capitalized on it. But the youth set—post-Boomers and Generation Xers—represented the company's largest opportunity for growth and, unfortunately for Levi Strauss & Co., many of these younger consumers perceived the classic 501 blue jeans with the little red tag as the pants *their parents wore*. In addition, competition from The Gap had become deadly serious and designer labels returned with a vengeance. Slipping customer demand led to manufacturing cuts in 1997. Levi Strauss & Co. shut eleven U.S. plants and offered 6,400 employees a generous $200 million severance package that was a sign of the deep pain felt within the company.

With $7 billion in annual sales, Levi Strauss & Co. was still a giant, the market leader. But something had to change, so the company began rethinking its traditional mass-marketing campaigns and refocused its energies on more consumer-driven approaches. Shank says the company realized it had to shift its marketing efforts toward the trendsetters who would eventually influence the rest of the marketplace. Although these groups represented a smaller portion of sales by volume, the company believed that focusing its marketing efforts on them would prove the best strategy for recultivating its youthful, dynamic image. The Baby Boomers were already giving the company a high share of their business, but their children weren't. So, as if traveling on a temporal Mobius strip, Levi Strauss & Co. circled back to capture the *next* young generation.

The company's efforts to appeal to younger consumers were abetted by a rare stroke of luck: In a stunning demonstration of cultural recycling, the children of the nineties rejected the cosmopolitanism of the seventies and eighties and turned to the sixties for inspiration. What could be more sixties than blue jeans? The company's first steps toward this new youth market led through predictable marketing territory: sponsoring music events, researching nightclubs, using Web technology to establish a link with college-age consumers. Levi Strauss & Co. also wisely decided to leverage its knowledge of mass customization to create new products for the new youth market.

What exactly is *mass customization?* In the case of Levi Strauss & Co., it meant taking what first appeared to be a giant step backward. For years the company manufactured jeans by cutting fabric 60-ply—that is, by taking 60 layers of fabric and cutting a single pattern across the entire stack. By the 1990s new technologies made it possible to cut jeans single-ply, or one at a time, with little loss of time. In effect, the lot size dropped from 60 to one.

Although the one-ply method itself was more costly, savings over the entire course of the selling process—from cotton ball to customer's closet—actually made it cost-efficient to sell the blue jeans one pair at a time!

The ability to mass-customize enabled Levi Strauss & Co. to start building Learning Relationships with its customers. The company could now tailor products to meet individual needs, but only if the customer was willing to make the investment in time and energy to tell the company how to do it.

In 1995, Levi Strauss & Co. rolled out its first personalization program, Personal Pair, for women customers. The idea was simple: The company would manufacture blue jeans that fit a woman's exact measurements. Personal Pair was available at 56 Original Levi Stores in North America, and it became an immediate hit. Personal Pair jeans weren't 100 percent customized, in the sense that they weren't made from scratch based on one customer's unique measurements. Instead women tried on various jeans to establish which fit was closest to their own and the results of this fitting session were sent electronically to the factory. Personal Pair illustrated the

"Lego block" principle of mass customization. Mass customization requires several—perhaps hundreds or thousands—of predesigned parts or modules that can be assembled into "unique" configurations that meet an individual customer's needs. In this case, more than 10,000 blue jean patterns were stored electronically, and when an order came in, the best-fitting design was chosen. In this way women still found variety they couldn't get on store shelves. The pants seemed truly customized—so Personal Pair jeans were sold at a price 20 percent higher than other Levi's jeans. To its delight, the company found that many customers, after receiving their first Personal Pair, would immediately pick up the phone and reorder three more pairs—again, all at a price 20 percent higher than the price for pre-made jeans.

A primary question about the Personal Pair program was whether it would be profitable. Would the savings in inventory—you wouldn't have to store thousands of pairs in hundreds of variations on shelves—balance the higher costs of the single-ply manufacturing? The answer was yes. But the real surprise came when the company realized customization was *increasing the Lifetime Value of each Levi's jeans customer.* "One of the statistics that has blown me away," Shank recalls, "was that every time we communicated with a customer who had previously purchased a Personal Pair, saying 'Would you like another pair?' the percentage who responded positively was incredible." In fact, Levi Strauss & Co. found that almost 40 percent of previous buyers were willing to buy another pair, a huge increase over the typical repeat purchase rate of 10 to 12 percent.

It's worth remembering that the cost of generating these repeat sales dropped to practically zero, because the customers were doing all the work and still paying the same premium. Clearly, it was in the company's best interest to get customers to want different things, because by catering to diverse needs it would be able to make customers more loyal and increase profit margins.

Then Levi Strauss & Co. found a second benefit: Customization was actually extending the life of certain products. How did this happen? From a product's perspective, it's a tough world out there. In 1995, the same year Personal Pair jeans became available, more than 21,000 new consumer products of all kinds were introduced on store shelves in the United States. (This compares to 5,700 new consumer products in 1983.) The life cycle of these new products, once as long as five years, now can be as short as six weeks. Eight out of ten product introductions fail.

"Manufacturers like us tend to produce a product, take it to market, and offer it for sale," Shank says. "And as it begins to diminish in life cycle, we discontinue manufacturing it because we can't store an infinite amount of inventory. And so as products become less popular, we discontinue them." The problem with this natural selection process, Shank says, is that good products often die—even if they have a loyal following among the company's most valuable or most growable customers. This is how mass marketers, in their race to please everybody all of the time, often end up *losing customers they were once able to satisfy.* For Levi Strauss & Co., mass customization turned the situation around. If a customer loved the fit of a pair of jeans she purchased two years ago, she could now recreate those pants—even if the style had been discontinued.

EXTREME STYLES

The current youth market, which has embraced bell bottoms, straight legs, boot cut, hard fit, loose fit, baggy fit, relaxed fit—almost every wild and outlandish style of blue jeans imaginable—has sorely tested the stock management capabilities of retailers. At the same time, the sudden demand for fashion options offered Levi Strauss & Co. an opportunity to expand its customization program to include new and different types of customers. In 1997, Personal Pair was joined by Original Spin, and by the end of 1998 Levi Strauss had combined both programs under the Original Spin banner.

Original Spin employs a Web site to provide a menu of choices: color, zipper or buttons, fabric, bottom opening, widths of knee etc. Customers can now customize the look of their jeans—in essence, build a pair of jeans. Customers can make appointments at any Levi's store in North America to be measured for pants that fit exactly, or they can have the pants cut in any of a variety of styles. Shank says early sales results are promising. The company plans to expand customization programs even further by potentially offering a Favorite Pair option. The program would enable a customer to re-create a favorite pair of pants—a pair that is getting threadbare, perhaps, or maybe a pair of pants that doesn't fit as well as it used to because the customer has gained weight. It doesn't even matter if the original pair of pants were made by competitors. Any "favorite" could be re-created to meet a customer's expressed needs.

Mass customization vaulted Levi Strauss & Co. into a position where it could build Learning Relationships with its end-users. "It gives us an incredible opportunity to begin managing customer relationships," Shank says. "A few years ago, we were selling about a million pairs of pants a day around the world—and we just didn't know who was actually buying them. We didn't know their names or addresses. Sure, we could look at statistical data in terms of size, SKU and fit specifications on a mass basis, but it wasn't granular enough for us to do much with, other than replicate the product that was selling and discontinue the product that wasn't."

The program also enables Levi Strauss & Co. to attract new customers and then hold on to them without resorting to discounts. Many companies try to win new customers with low introductory prices, eroding their margins in the process. For Shank, a mass-customized product provided the ticket out of the dilemma. He reasoned—correctly—that many people tend to buy blue jeans on the basis of fit, not price. What better way to ensure a good fit than by mass customizing? And what kind of customer would expect a discount on a pair of *customized* blue jeans? Soon the company had the best of both worlds: highly satisfied customers, paying a premium.

But mass customization has yet another benefit for the company: it allows the firm to offer a nearly infinite "inventory" of sizes and styles, without incurring any of the exorbitant inventory costs it would face in a nondigital world.

"Electronically," says Shank, "we can pretty much offer you anything you need. Take something as simple as waist size. In the men's business, somebody years ago decided that men grew in two-inch increments. Every store I go to has 30s, 32s, 34s and 36s. And what happens if you're in between?" The reason for that system, Shank says, is inventory control. "It's a challenge. How do you manage all that inventory with so many permutations? But if you store product electronically—that is, you don't make the pants until somebody orders them—it can be accomplished very easily. We can do it in quarter-inch increments if you want. Just tell us what you want, give us your credit card number and we'll put them in the mail to you.

"I've met people at cocktail parties," Shank says, "and when they find out where I work, they come out of their shoes with a blatant statement that, 'Oh, Levi's jeans don't fit.' And it's normally based on an experience some twenty years ago when they went to a store, tried on one pair of pants, and it didn't fit. And therefore they have cursed the brand forever." Shank laughs. "Well, if I could just have an opportunity to investigate that relationship with those people . . . they could become the most loyal customers in the world. I think once they find that you do fit, they'll stay with you forever."

And what about the badge value of owning a pair of blue jeans with a little red Levi's tag? Will customization enhance or erode the venerable brand? "I think brands exist in the minds and hearts of the consumer," Shank says. "The consumer has become sophisticated far beyond anything that we used to know when we first went to market. For a brand to remain relevant and to resonate with the consumer . . ." Shank pauses. "You must enhance the relationship by responding to consumer needs."

Based on its recent experiences in the marketplace, Levi Strauss & Co. is in the midst of major organizational change to focus on customer needs. "It's a new frontier for us," Shank adds. "Thirty-second television commercials alone won't get the job done anymore." The new business model, which the company dubs "consumer-focused brand management," calls for tightly structured brand groups that draw from centralized support services. Brands are matched against specific customer needs. Portions of the Levi's brand, for example, will focus on the clothing needs of youth. The Dockers and Slates brands will focus on the needs of young adults.

"We don't believe that we will sell all products one-to-one," Shank says, "nor do we believe we can rely on the mass marketing model alone. So we also make products as we have historically and put them on shelves in the community and people come in and buy what they want." Levi Strauss & Co., like any smart business, is hedging its bets. It also knows that different customers will require different approaches. Not *every* customer needs to be a one-to-one customer.

Shank predicts that personalized clothing will account for 25 percent of sales within five years and says Levi Strauss & Co. plans to expand its customization programs aggressively. The company recently decided to open two online stores to sell Levi's jeans and Dockers khakis. The move is aimed at boosting awareness of the company's wide line of products, opening a new distribution channel and countering The Gap's and other vertically integrated retailers' growing presence on the Web. The company's new sites, Levi.com and Dockers.com, also are likely to vacuum up huge amounts of potentially valuable information, ranging from customer preferences to unedited feedback.

Just as innovation and price points can be imitated, customization can be mimicked too. But there is an important difference. "We think the switching costs are going to be greater," Shank says. "If we can satisfy you with 'our brand' and continue to build it in different variations with different fabrics and color palettes to your satisfaction, then it's going to be more and more difficult to depart from the franchise." Levi's Original Spin and Personal Pair programs vividly demonstrate how a company can customize products and services to retain customers, even in the face of intense competition.

These efforts are an excellent example of the "consumer direct" sales model, in which manufacturers bypass traditional intermediaries and sell goods directly to end-users. Moving to consumer direct can raise channel conflicts, but it also creates enormous opportunities. "In a consumer-direct scenario, we own the customer relationship," says Janie Ligon, vice president, Direct to Consumer, at Levi Strauss. "We learn about the customer, we fulfill the customer's needs in a cost-effective way and we deliver the finished goods right to the customer's doorstep. That's a win-win situation."

The day may come when every manufacturer offers custom-made clothing that hugs every curve and still lets you sit down. If Gordon Shank and his team have anything to say about it, Levi Strauss & Co. will get there first. And he's betting that once a customer goes through the process once, she won't want to start all over again somewhere else.

Shank firmly believes the customer relationships of tomorrow will be as satisfying to both the buyer and seller as the friendships he made while driving through the Canadian hinterlands in his Monte Carlo. Back then, he was a salesman with a popular product. Today, he's a guy with a strategic vision: Get the customer to help design the clothes and you'll have a customer for life.

Company: 1-800-FLOWERS
(WESTBURY, NEW YORK)

Pioneer: *Jim McCann, president and CEO*
Lesson: *At a genuine 1to1 enterprise, technology should be used to create and empower a culture of customer service. When it is, it will be difficult to determine what counts most for the company's success—technology or culture.*

Long before he ever sold a flower, Jim McCann learned about the importance of one-to-one relationships. One such relationship saved his life. After graduating from college and putting in a brief stint as a bartender in Queens, McCann took on the toughest job he would ever face: managing a group home for troubled boys in nearby Rockaway Beach. "That's where I learned you have a better chance of reaching your goals if you communicate and interact with people as individuals, not as groups."

After getting some good advice from one of the Mari-anist monks whose order ran the home, McCann began reaching out to the residents—one at a time. One lonely youth, named Elwin, had no family to cheer him on when he played scholastic football. So McCann became the boy's one-man cheering section, attending games and events all over New York City to show his support. Grad-ually, they got to know each other and became friends. One night, after an argument over a TV program, an-other youth, Raymond, attacked McCann with a baseball bat. McCann recalls the incident in his autobiography, *Stop and Sell the Roses:*

Just as [Raymond] swung the bat I flew out of the chair and hit the floor. CRASSHH! The chair ex-ploded in smithereens. I remember seeing a wild, mad dog look in his eyes and thinking, "That's it, Jim, this is where the story ends." I tried . . . to get out of the way, but Raymond was faster than I was. . . .

Then Elwin was coming—he leapt off the couch and, as Raymond was at the apex of his windup, El-win ripped into his side with a tackle that drove him into the wall. . . . When I calmed down, I reflected on what had happened . . . in some sense, Elwin felt indebted to me. It wasn't a money thing, but it was nonetheless a debt. My going to those games had been an investment in our relationship. I was hoping that my return on investment would be a motivated kid doing better in school. I got that, but I also got someone who saved my life.

McCann never forgot that lesson in relationship building. Now, as the high-profile CEO of 1-800-FLOWERS, McCann still sees personal relationships as the true measure of success. "The floral business is, by nature, all about relationships," says McCann. "At 1-800-FLOWERS, our core philosophy—whether we are talking about employees, business partners or customers—is predicated on building one-to-one relationships."

McCann was quick to see the role information technology would play in creating a 1to1 enterprise. While his competitors dropped huge amounts of cash on advertising, McCann steadily funneled his company's profits back into the technology infrastructure that would enable him to capture and organize as much customer data as possible. This investment paid handsome dividends in improved operational efficiency and higher levels of customer loyalty.

"We have the capability to identify each and every one of our customers and their relationship with our products and services. We know who our customers are, and how often they order via the telephone, via the Internet, via our stores or via our catalogs. Understanding our customers' buying patterns allows us to control our product distribution, inventory and spoilage. It also gives us the opportunity to cultivate a one-to-one relationship with each customer."

These 1to1 relationships, in turn, result in more successful direct marketing efforts. "For example, we can distribute a targeted direct mail piece to only those customers we know are most likely to purchase a specific product during a promotion. This drastically cuts down on the overhead of our direct marketing efforts while generating more customer participation and increased revenue," says McCann.

1-800-FLOWERS was one of the first online retailers to recognize the full potential of the Internet as a tool for continuous interactivity. "We use the Internet to correspond directly with the people who comprise our growing list of online customers. Using targeted e-mail communication, for example, we can successfully communicate with customers and drive their business to any of our four channels. Electronic commerce accounts for over 10 percent of our revenues, and this area is our fastest-growing revenue stream. It may seem impersonal, but it's not. We have had *great* success in developing one-to-one relationships on the Web," McCann reports gleefully.

"Extending one-to-one marketing philosophies into our interactive sales channel has also brought us significant growth in our traditional sales channels. By visiting our virtual world, our customers can learn all about our products, services, promotions, store locations and special features. At the same time, the Web allows us to reinforce our brand position and to identify and address the issues facing our customers," he notes.

The company's Web site, *1800flowers.com,* now features a "real time" customer service chat option. By clicking on an icon, customers can communicate directly with a live customer service representative. "As e-commerce pioneers we have noticed that the Internet consumers are beginning to expect the same level of service from their retailers that they receive in the traditional retail environment," says McCann. "Online retailers who do not deliver a seamless operation across all of their retail channels run the risk of losing significant market share to their competition," he predicts.

Training and education play a significant role in the one-to-one process at 1-800-FLOWERS. "All of our associates are schooled in the fine art of relationship building," says McCann. "We've even created an in-house program we call Floraversity. The extensive training classes offered through Floraversity give our employees the skills they need to create one-to-one relationships with our customers. Training has become our most important way to educate employees about the importance of relationship building and to spread our core message throughout the company."

As a veteran of the rough-and-tumble neighborhoods of Queens, McCann knows that money remains an indisputably powerful motivator. "Our model of compensation is under review," he says. In the future, sales associates will be rewarded on the basis of their ability to perform in a 1to1 atmosphere.

"It will actually begin with the recruitment and hiring processes. A screening test will ensure that we hire people who are best suited to thrive in a one-to-one environment. In addition to the change in hiring practice, 1-800-FLOWERS will incorporate a compensation model that will reward performance. Each associate in the company will know where he or she stands in terms of their compensation base, and they will also know how their compensation can be positively affected by their performance, which will include attitude, ability and contribution to the one-to-one environment."

McCann embraces his role as a 1to1 pioneer with missionary zeal. He holds a quarterly management communications meeting with all of the company's managers and supervisors. An outside communications consultant also attends the meeting to help keep things on track. McCann holds monthly conference calls with all managers and supervisors across the organization. To ensure that all employees have equal access to the boss, McCann has created an internal communications program titled "Dear Jim."

"The 'Dear Jim' program allows every one of our 2,000 employees an opportunity to ask me a question directly. We have created and distributed business reply mail cards, with an adhesive tape sealer to ensure privacy, which allows a direct line of communication between every employee and me. A component of the 'Dear Jim' program is a monthly letter called 'Jim's Update.' It's distributed to all our employees and answers questions of widespread interest."

McCann sees the ability to function in a 1to1 world as necessary to his company's very survival. "I would say, historically speaking, the most successful companies are those that have always placed customer service before product service. I'll admit it is a fine line that must be drawn here, but if a company doesn't focus on the customer, at least equally as much as it focuses on its product line, then that company is flirting with disaster. Because a competitor can always duplicate your product, the difference comes down to how you treat your customers. Consider what a famous food critic once observed about restaurants: Is your favorite restaurant the one that serves the best food? No. It's the one where the proprietor and staff know your name."

Company: First Union
(CHARLOTTE, NORTH CAROLINA)

Pioneer: *Jack Antonini, executive vice-president of consumer banking*

Lesson: *Silos are bad. Integration is good. Simple, obvious—but very difficult to accomplish.*

Jack Antonini remembers the first time he ever went into a bank. Holding his father's hand, he looked up at the vaulted ceilings and the marble pillars. He saw the tellers in their cages, the armed guard and the polished steel door of the walk-in safe. Antonini was the son of an immigrant factory worker and the grandson of a coal miner. The bank in his hometown of Grand Rapids, Michigan, seemed like a forbidden temple from the movies. "It was awesome. It was huge. But it was also very cold and very impersonal and very intimidating," he recalls.

Now the head of the Consumer Banking Group at First Union, Antonini finds the memory of that old bank useful. "My plan is to make our bank as *un*intimidating and as personal as we can possibly make it. I'd like people to think of us as a friendly neighbor down the street."

Perhaps to a greater degree than anyone else in the industry, Antonini is perfectly positioned to achieve this vision. Even so, projecting the image of a genuinely helpful bank is only one small part of the battle. Building relationships is the real challenge. The measure of Antonini's success will depend largely on his ability to improve overall profitability, not by cutting costs or growing market share, but by increasing the profitability of the customers he already has.

Phrased in the language of the 1to1 marketer, Antonini must grow his *Share of Customer.* He must capture more financial business from each customer, across all the bank's different product lines, and over as long a period as possible. He has to grow his customers bigger and keep them longer.

In the retail banking business, customer loyalty and "multi-lineness" are known to be highly correlated. For example, at a typical U.S. bank nearly half the customers with only a single checking account and no other product line will leave within a year. A third of a bank's customers who have only a time deposit product, such as a CD, will leave within a year. But only 10 percent of customers who have both a checking account *and* a time deposit account will leave within a year. For customers with checking, time deposit and mortgage products, annual attrition drops to just 2 percent, and for customers with checking, time deposit, mortgage and credit card products, the attrition rate is less than 1 percent.

What this means is that, if Antonini can figure out how to sell more lines of products to a customer, he not only is making that customer more profitable to the bank in the short term, but he is likely also extending that customer's tenure as a customer. But it won't be easy.

BIG-TIME VERTICALS

Since 1997, Antonini has been responsible for managing First Union's mortgage, home equity, auto finance, PC remote and telephone banking operations, as well as all card products and the bank's Knowledge Based Marketing program. Deposit products were recently moved under his aegis, giving him the broadest possible mandate across the bank's array of consumer offerings. When he accepted the job, each of the bank's consumer product lines functioned autonomously.

Antonini recalls the "bad old days" with a grimace. "There was a CEO at the mortgage company, there was a CEO at the home equity bank, there was a separate auto financing business. These were big-time vertical silos. They had everything they needed. They had their own human resources, services and processing operations. Each vertical silo reported its own profit and loss. And you could have sold off any one of these units and they would have continued to operate perfectly well as independent entities. When you're organized by product, it's very easy to see what your costs are and how many units you've sold. But as a result, we ended up with 43 percent of our customers using *only one* of our products."

What's more, a silo organization often engages in plainly irrational practices with respect to individual customers. This was true at First Union as well. For example, under the old table of organization, each business unit had its own credit decision engine, and there was no requirement that these decisions had to be related, even when they related to the same exact customer. "We had about five different systems," says Antonini. "So not only did we have to pay for it five times, we also had five times as many systems people as we needed. And on top of that we had inconsistent credit decisions for the same customer! We had customers getting letters saying they were pre-approved for a credit card, but when they went into a branch to get a car loan, they were turned down. You don't have to be a credit expert to know that's dumb."

Or to take another example, the bank's home equity loan products were spread over several different business lines, and this required potential customers to shop through four different channels within the company to find the best deal. Says Antonini: "Once again, not only did this mean paying to maintain four different decision engines and four different documentation systems, but to our customers it was ridiculous!"

So Antonini reorganized the Consumer Banking Group into three major functional areas—Product, Process, and Channel. *Product* includes lending, credit cards and deposits. *Process* includes marketing, risk management, financial management, human resources and operations/technology. *Channel* includes every point of customer contact—the bank's financial centers (branches), First Union Direct (telephone banking), Online Banking and ATMs.

All three areas were arranged to encourage customer-focused activities while discouraging behavior that was purely product-centric. In other words, the bank rethought any activity that might throw roadblocks in the way of individualized customer service *across the enterprise.*

To do this Antonini pulled some of the process work away from the individual business units and reassigned it to expert teams that would serve the needs of the enterprise. "Even for different loan products, a lot of the origination processing is the same—you've got to pull a credit report, calculate debt-to-income ratios, work your way through the numbers. So we decided to pull that expertise together into one area. That way, we can leverage the technology to provide an outstanding experience for the customer."

The result of this reorganization was that First Union could now take a rational view of each of its individual customers, no matter how many products the customer had. And this, in turn, allowed the bank to begin managing its customers, rather than just administering its products. "Now," says Antonini, "it's your own individual credit qualifications that determine what your product looks like, and not the channel you came through."

EINSTEIN HELPS OUT

First Union's most important line of defense against a resurgence of product-centric behaviors is Einstein, a proprietary software system that enables the bank's front-line personnel to choose from a wide range of options when dealing with a customer. "We called it Einstein because we wanted each customer to think they're talking to a genius whenever they talk to one of our people. It shows us at a glance the full relationship between us and the customer, including the accounts they've closed out.

It also displays the overall value of the relationship and calculates the profitability of that individual customer. And based upon all that information, it empowers the customer representative to make highly individualized decisions on the spot."

For example, the customer rep would know instantly whether to override the bank's policy on overdrafts and waive the standard penalty. Rather than agonize over a few dollars, it makes perfect business sense to differentiate between highly valuable customers who might just decide to take their business elsewhere, and chronic writers of bad checks who might indeed pose a greater financial risk to the bank than they are worth. Einstein lets the bank's front-liners escape from the "all-or-nothing" scenarios required by policy-driven processes, and instead deliver real-time, individualized solutions that are far more likely to keep valuable customers happy.

You Are What You Measure

Antonini says that the primary objective of First Union's direct channels is to ensure an outstanding customer experience, and therefore "we quantify that experience. For example, in our telephone center we used to measure the average speed to answer a call and how long the operator stayed on the phone, that kind of stuff. Now we're measuring how well we take care of the customer. Were we able to solve the customer's problem in one phone call? Was the customer satisfied?"

The bank generally surveys customers to gather feedback, either by mail or telephone, within forty-eight hours of a contact. If urgent problems are uncovered, the appropriate manager is informed via e-mail or phone. Survey results are published and distributed in a monthly report.

Antonini also has what he calls a "rapid deployment" team to gather feedback on new programs. Not long ago, when the bank began a push to migrate more routine transactions to its ATMs, the call center began receiving complaints from customers who were depositing out-of-town checks in the machines. By law, the bank is required to tell customers how long it's going to take for checks to clear. By glancing at the check, a teller can let the customer know how many days to wait before writing checks against the deposit. An ATM has no way of doing this, so customers were often unaware that their out-of-town checks were being held. "By now they've already written checks against that deposit," Antonini explains. "They're calling up and saying, 'Are my checks going to bounce?' or 'How could this happen?' We had one customer who deposited a First Union check in an ATM expecting to get an immediate credit. But when the check was processed, our system read the routing number, saw it was an out-of-town check and put a hold on it. The customer called up in a panic and, of course, we took the hold off the check. Then we went back and changed the process so that First Union checks would not be placed on hold and credit would be available that evening."

Antonini's crew saw First Union's recent merger with Philadelphia-based CoreStates Financial Corp. as an opportunity to launch a dialogue with CoreStates customers. This dialogue would not only serve as an introduction but also reveal potentially valuable information about the preferences and habits of CoreStates customers. "We have a magazine called *Financial Solutions* and we designed one issue uniquely for CoreStates customers so we could explain to them what their accounts would look like after the merger, what First Union was planning to do, who they could call to get problems resolved, all those things they would need to know," says Antonini.

"And we included a survey with the magazine. We asked them attitudinal questions, such as, 'How do you feel about ATMs? Do you really hate them, or do you find them convenient?' We also asked them if they feel they have effectively been planning and saving for their financial future and other questions like that. Following up on the survey, we put together a customized letter that we sent to each individual customer who completed it. If they really hated ATMs, for example, the letter told them where all the nearest branches were located. If they said they didn't really feel as though they had adequately planned for their kids' college education, we suggested they make an appointment with one of the financial specialists at their nearby branch who would be able to help them with planning. Each letter was tailored to the individual customer and aimed squarely at their unique needs, based on the feedback they gave us. The customers, by the way, reacted very positively. Some said they had been afraid of what would happen when First Union took over, but the letters showed them they had nothing to fear and that, in fact, we were bringing better service than they had received in the past."

INVEST IN LOYALTY

First Union is still in the early stages of developing a precise method for measuring the Lifetime Value of its individual customers to determine their potential profitability over many, many years of transactions. But the bank has moved forward into differentiating its customers by value to ensure that it's not investing too much—or too little—to build customer loyalty. "We have what we call our Five Star Customer, which is a very profitable customer with whom we have a very strong relationship. With this customer, we need to make sure we're taking all the right steps in terms of pricing, product offers, special services, etc. Then we have the Rising Star Customer. With the Rising Star, we realize that we don't yet have the depth or breadth we'd like to have in our relationship with that customer, but we *could* have a highly valuable relationship if we handle all the details properly." (These categories, Five Star and Rising Star, correspond to what we call MVCs and MGCs—or Most Valuable Customers and Most Growable Customers. See *The One to One Fieldbook,* p. 59.)

Rising Stars will be offered a series of First Union products that are likely to match their current financial needs. One such product is CAP, the bank's nickname for its Capital Management Account. CAP customers agree to maintain a $15,000 minimum balance and pay an annual fee. In return, they get discounts on commissions when they trade stocks, "instant credit" margin loans, unlimited free checking, no-fee Visa Gold credit and debit cards, customizable monthly statements to simplify expense tracking, a free safe deposit box and other perks. CAP customers also are assigned a Personal Investment Counselor for investment advice and receive *Portfolio Edge,* a quarterly newsletter explaining CAP features, any recent service enhancements and investment tips.

The bank has designed enough flexibility into the CAP product to make it easily customizable. "If we're marketing a CAP account to a Rising Star and we see she already has a credit card with us, maybe we'll offer her a home equity loan at a preferred rate. If we know she's got a car loan, for example, we may offer to refinance the loan because rates are probably a whole lot lower than they were when she first got the loan. If we can save her $30 a month on her car loan, we'll do it. In the case of younger customers, we might try to get them started with a CAP1 account, which allows a lower minimum balance ($5,000) and offers a slightly less robust service set. Our approach will depend entirely on the unique needs of the individual customer."

Antonini acknowledges that not all Rising Star Customers are destined to become Five Star Customers. Nevertheless, the bank will make the effort to lay the foundation for long-term relationships with customers identified as Rising Stars. "If, after two years, we're still beating our heads against the wall and we're getting nowhere, then we'll shift gears and focus our attentions on somebody else who's a better opportunity," Antonini says.

Life events play a significant role in the bank's efforts to build customer relationships. "If someone's got a child going off to college, we provide a variety of different financing mechanisms to pay for it all. We also provide a checking account for the child, as well as access to our online banking services. We can arrange for funds to be deposited automatically in the child's account, once a month or however often the parents want to do it. We'll provide a debit card so the child has access to the cash. We'll give the kid a credit card to use in emergencies, one that would allow him to buy tickets home, that sort of thing. We'll try to link as many service offerings to a particular life event—a child going off to college, a family buying a new home or moving to a new town—as we possibly can."

All this raises an interesting question, one we will return to again and again: Why is First Union one of the few banks to adopt such an aggressive customer management program? It is such an obvious idea. It's so simple, and so undeniably beneficial to the bank.

One answer to this question has to do with what we said earlier, about pre-existing circumstances. Every business evolves within its own environment, with its own set of restrictions and traditions. In the case of retail banking, the industry has always been heavily regulated. Until just twenty years ago, government agencies told a bank what products it could offer and what rates it could charge. "As a result, you had to become a very efficient transactor," says Antonini. "In the old days, a 1 percent return on assets was considered high performance. So you made money by being efficient, by processing more transactions more quickly than your competition. The strange thing is that, while the regulatory environment has changed drastically, most banks continue to focus on transactions and haven't stopped to think about customer relations. They're still trying to figure out how to move more people through the teller lines. What we're doing is considered very radical in the banking world."

But a better answer to the question of why all banks aren't already trying to do what First Union is doing is simply that *old habits die hard.*

In the Era of Mass Marketing, nearly *every* business organized itself into vertical silos along distinct product lines, because it was too difficult and inefficient to organize any other way. But in organizing itself, a company hard-wires its controls, measurements and other processes into the enterprise, and for traditional marketing these processes are virtually all product-centric. Consequently they not only require a facilitating product-centric organization, but over time the organization and the processes generate a supporting, product-centric culture at the firm—and this culture will be "blind" to any alternatives.

That's the principal reason that pushing out in the 1to1 direction is a pioneering activity to begin with. And it can be lonely out there on the frontier.

Thought Generator
Using Technology

Remember how Odysseus had himself tied to the mast so he wouldn't succumb to the irresistible song of the Sirens? And how he filled the ears of his shipmates with beeswax so they wouldn't hear the song? That's sort of the way many marketing executives have been dealing with technology for a long time. Odysseus, to his credit, had a workable plan and the personnel to carry it out successfully.

Do *you* have a plan for automating your marketing functions and do *you* have the right people on board to help you?

Does your customer information reside in the "silos" of different business divisions? What steps can you take to integrate information across these silos and make it available to anyone who comes into contact with a customer? First Union created "Einstein," but shrink-wrapped, off-the-shelf solutions are evolving rapidly. Who at your organization tracks the development of these solutions?

How could you use information technology to jump-start Learning Relationships with your best customers?

If you're easily embarrassed, you might consider skipping the next question. Did you ask your customers what they wanted in your Web site before building one? If you said no, don't feel bad. A recent survey showed fewer than one in ten companies actually talks with its customers before launching a Web site.

In retrospect, can you think of an additional function you could add to your own Web site *tomorrow* that would improve your organization's ability to manage customer relationships?

Now imagine this scenario: You're a business

executive, manager, or entrepreneur. You're also a modern-day Rip Van Winkle. You go to sleep tonight and wake up twenty years from now. When you wake up, you find that just about everyone is hooked into the Web, using it constantly. They're not connecting from PCs, but from cell phones, pagers, cars, televisions, wristwatches, whatever. They're using the Web to shop, work, learn, gather information, entertain themselves and communicate with friends around the world. What would *your* organization's Web site have to look like in this new world? Rip Van Winkle might go back to sleep—you can't. So what's your first step? How will you begin the journey toward a personalized, automated Web site?

Here's a final thought before leaving this chapter: Although brand marketing and 1to1 marketing seem to represent opposite poles, Levi Strauss relies on brand strength to drive its mass customization efforts. What would be the role for your own organization's brand, if you were to mass customize your product or service?

Please e-mail your responses to
usingtechnology@1to1.com

3

Organization, Culture and Change

As an organization evolves from a traditional, product-focused enterprise to a customer-focused, customer-driven enterprise, it will need a new infrastructure to support the processes and behaviors of 1to1 marketing.

Chances are you'll be tearing down walls (literally and figuratively), buying more computers, and retraining employees to create an environment in which teamwork flourishes, communication is facilitated, and more sophisticated information tools allow the entire organization to make decisions with a more customer-centered point of view. User-friendly data mining tools will allow your managers, at a variety of levels throughout the company, to spot previously unnoticed trends, hidden connections and potential relationships, and to act on this knowledge in a more and more autonomous fashion.

In our experience, the most difficult part of making
this transition is usually not acquiring and installing the
technologies required, but adapting the organization and
its people to use them. What is happening is not the
acceleration of business-the-way-it-always-has-been, but
a major change in the way business *is*. The cultural and
organizational obstacles posed are immense.

It's one thing to have an idea about how the enterprise
ought to manage its customer relationships and measure
its effectiveness, but it's another thing entirely to navigate
through this transition successfully.

Here's some excellent advice from General McDermott: "Make sure the people who are going to implement
the plan are involved in the planning process. Let them
discuss all the possible glitches, agree on a course of action and run a test."

In reality, McDermott did more than merely include
key managers in his strategy sessions. He treated them as
valued colleagues and cherished comrades.

"We were like the Knights of the Round Table," says
McDermott, smiling as he remembers the men and
women who worked alongside him at USAA. "I was not
an authoritarian commander, I was a leader. We used a
'round table' approach to make sure everyone who was
going to be involved in the implementation was also involved in the planning and discussion. That way, everyone in the management group was fully informed and
singing from the same hymnal."

If the image of gallant knights in shining armor strikes
you as too idealized, consider an earthier image from the
nineteenth century. Before laying out a new campaign for

his senior staff, General Ulysses S. Grant would explain the plan to one of his dullest enlisted soldiers. Not until Grant was satisfied that he had successfully managed to communicate his intentions to this dim-witted soldier would he show the plan to his staff.

Company: USAA (SAN ANTONIO, TEXAS)

Pioneer: Brigadier General Robert McDermott, former CEO of USAA

Lesson: Transforming a company from product–oriented silos into an integrated, 1to1 enterprise requires a thoughtful, comprehensive approach, involving not just marketing but the organization and its culture as well.

One reason Jack Antonini felt comfortable leading First Union into the 1to1 marketing frontier was that he learned firsthand how to build and run a customer-focused financial service from one of the industry's greatest living legends, General Robert McDermott. McDermott became a father figure in the field of customer relationship management in the 1970s and '80s, by transforming a stodgy, bureaucratic mutual insurance company, USAA, into what amounts to one of today's most successful icons of one-to-one marketing.

In the saga of CRM and 1to1 marketing, General Robert McDermott, former World War II fighter pilot and the first permanent dean at the U. S. Air Force Academy, plays the role of Obi-Wan Kenobi. The general not only served as mentor to Jack Antonini and a host of other prominent bankers, he also created the first technology-enabled, customer-focused company in the financial services sector. His odyssey to the top job at USAA was filled with unexpected twists and turns. His father played trombone for the Boston Symphony and young Robert was trained as a musician. But he chose to attend West Point and graduated in 1943, just as the Allies were beginning to turn the tide against the Axis powers in World War II.

McDermott flew 61 combat missions in a Lockheed P-38 Lightning, then considered America's state-of-the-art warplane. Fast and deadly, it was tricky to handle—especially if one of its two supercharged engines conked out. McDermott managed to tame the airplane and survive the war, garnering a Bronze Star and an Air Medal with Five Oak Leaf Clusters in the process. He spent a year working on General Dwight Eisenhower's staff, then went to Harvard for an MBA. After Harvard, he returned to West Point, where he taught economics. He also wrote and edited books on insurance, personal finance and national security. At the academy, McDermott became known as one of those rare professors who possessed both scholarly brilliance *and* the ability to teach.

Early in his tenure at West Point, the Korean conflict began, and McDermott noted with frustration that most of the nation's insurers hastily invoked war clauses to avoid paying life insurance claims filed by the dependents of soldiers killed in action. It had been the same in World War II—insurers quickly got off the hook by citing war clauses written into their life insurance policies. Thinking of the young cadets who sat in his classes, McDermott resolved that if he ever wound up in the insurance business, he would make sure that *his* company acted more honorably. But he would have to wait eighteen years to get the chance.

By 1954, McDermott's reputation as a forceful but humane educator had spread beyond West Point. The pilot-turned-scholar drew the attention of the top brass at the newly minted Air Force Academy in Colorado. The Air Force, which was less than a decade old, was struggling to fill its officer corps with individuals with enough education to master the emerging technologies of aerospace warfare. The thin, dry air of Colorado was the perfect atmosphere to nurture a new breed of officers who thought—and fought—at supersonic speed.

McDermott was assigned to the fledgling academy, where he promptly introduced what was, back then, a very radical concept: Because each cadet is a unique human being with a unique set of talents and intellectual capabilities, each cadet should be treated differently on an academic basis. "Before I came along, everybody took the same prescribed curriculum. But the important thing about students is their *differences,* not their sameness. God made us all *different,*" says McDermott. "As teacher, or parents or supervisors, our job is to help people discover their talents and develop them."

McDermott's vision of a service academy that celebrated individuality contrasted sharply with the regimentation cultures that had developed at both Annapolis and West Point ("one hundred years of tradition unhampered by progress"). But he won the support of his superiors, who understood that the entire reason for creating the Air Force as a separate arm of the service in the first place was to allow it to develop a culture that would be appropriate to the unique technology of air and space.

Over the next five years the Air Force Academy evolved with surprising speed into a top-notch college. McDermott, who had been appointed the academy's first permanent dean of faculty in 1959, was given the lion's share of credit for developing the school's highly successful academic program. By 1968, McDermott was ready for a new challenge. He found it at the United Services Automobile Association in San Antonio, Texas.

DROWNING IN PAPER

USAA was founded in 1922 by twenty-five Army officers who needed auto insurance but couldn't buy it at a fair price. Back in those days soldiers were considered bad risks—they moved around a lot and local companies often would not cover them. So the officers formed a mutual company to provide reciprocal insurance for one another. Over time, the little company grew and, by 1968, USAA had 650,000 customers (all current or former military officers) and $207 million in assets. Over the course of its growth, however, customer service had degenerated and USAA had developed a reputation for slovenly attention to detail. Constant internal bickering, low morale and high employee turnover plagued the company.

One of the first things McDermott noticed on an early visit to the company was a blizzard of paper covering every desk. "You can't imagine how much paper," he told the *Harvard Business Review.* "Stacks and piles and trays and baskets of it. And of course a lot of it got lost. On any given day, the chances were only 50–50 that we'd be able to put our hands on any particular file. . . . We constantly got letters and phone calls about poor service." The staff was so inundated by forms and documents that, when McDermott surreptitiously went around the office one night putting tiny marks on random pieces of paper on various desks, he discovered the next night that most of the paper had never moved!

Despite all these problems, McDermott accepted the company's offer to become its new president. Then he moved swiftly to steer USAA onto a new heading. His pioneering efforts to bring about this change illustrate why transforming a product-centric organization into a one-to-one enterprise requires an integrative, comprehensive approach. He clearly saw that changing the face his company showed its customers would involve a good deal more than simply altering the marketing strategy. He had to undo processes that had been hard-wired into USAA for decades, breaking down the old culture and constructing a new one virtually from scratch. His change plan had five components:

- Automation
- Attrition
- Reorganization
- Training and education
- Empowerment

Automation would allow him to create a digital, virtually paperless office. Also, it would enable the employees to provide greatly improved customer service because of the information that would be at their fingertips.

Attrition would allow him to replace a large portion of the embattled workforce with fresh faces recruited on the basis of their willingness to work in a customer-focused environment. Because of the company's high turnover, McDermott was able to accomplish this phase without resorting to the massive layoffs usually associated with corporate re-engineering.

Reorganization would break up the entrenched bureaucracies that had accumulated around departments such as accounting, claims and underwriting. Horizontal communication was all but nonexistent and nobody, it seemed, had a handle on the big picture.

Training and education would allow him to professionalize the company's employees to the point where they could make day-to-day decisions with minimum input from senior managers.

Empowerment would free the employees from the "production line" mentality that made it impossible for them to focus on customer issues.

"You train people and educate them and empower them so that, when a customer calls, they know all the answers and don't have to go running to a supervisor," says McDermott. "Think back to the military for a second: Do you think Eisenhower personally told the machine gunners where to aim? Certainly not. The soldiers knew their mission and were empowered to accomplish it."

McDermott began his crusade at USAA by creating five cross-functional groups and assigning a fifth of the company's customers to each group. Then he put the five groups into competition with each other to see which group could provide the best service and generate the highest levels of customer satisfaction. A large chunk of the company's budget was allocated to professional training that would help employees to rise through the ranks. It wasn't long before employees began viewing change and movement as *positives* to be embraced, rather than as *negatives* to be shunned. Employees were encouraged to apply for new positions and to move around as much as possible within the company. This perpetual motion, in turn, created a system in which key vacancies could be filled rapidly from within—sort of like the bombardier in a B-17 taking over for a wounded turret gunner. At the same time USAA was becoming more decentralized, it was achieving higher levels of flexibility and functional integration by notching up the quality of its workforce.

LEVERAGING TECHNOLOGY

McDermott's introduction of modern information technology not only brought greater efficiency and speed, it also gave front-line service people the capability to view a member's entire relationship with the company on a single screen. "We used technology for two purposes. One, to make it more convenient for the customer to do business with us. Two, to make us more efficient in serving the customer's needs. We got rid of, 'I'll get back to you in thirty days,' and replaced it with, 'I can handle your

problem right now.' We were the first financial services company to really get out there and start using information technology and telecommunications to make
doing business *easier for the customer and more efficient
for us.*"

One step at a time, McDermott's worldview—that
processes should serve human beings, not the other way
around—took hold and became the dominant force in the
company. Customers noticed the change and soon the
word spread—the company does limited advertising—
throughout the military branches. Under McDermott's
guidance, market penetration of active duty officers increased from 75 percent to 95 percent. But there still
remained a huge reservoir of untapped potential in officers *not* on active duty.

Since its inception, USAA had sold insurance only
to active or retired military officers. Any officer who
separated from the military prior to retirement became
ineligible. Although USAA had since modified its by-
laws to allow coverage for this sizable group, it had
made little effort to market a product to them. McDermott saw these uncovered officers as a pathway to increased market penetration and began actively courting
their business.

Now, it's important to remember that USAA calls its
customers "members" because, as a mutual insurance
company, its policyholders are its owners. McDermott
realized he would have to expand eligibility if he wanted
to grow the company beyond its original core market. In
1973 he began offering associate memberships to the

adult children of members. These "associate" members could buy automobile or home insurance but had no ownership in the firm. McDermott also convinced the company's board of directors to grant him permission to launch a consumer bank, issue credit cards, open a discount brokerage, and offer a selection of no-load mutual funds to the general public. The company is now made up of 85 subsidiaries and affiliates. It serves more than two million customers, manages assets of more than $45 billion, and was ranked 212th among U.S. corporations in terms of revenues.

In the face of all these financial measures of his success at USAA, McDermott says one of his most personally satisfying achievements is the way the company handled itself during Operation Desert Storm. Naturally, USAA has no war clause written into its life insurance policies. But what's remarkable is that the company continued to issue life policies to new officers as they were called to active duty to fight in the war, and it allowed existing members who were assigned combat roles to *increase their coverage.* Also, the company set up a hotline so that, if a member were killed during the war, the survivors would have a single point of contact to resolve questions about life insurance, property insurance, banking and investment management.

At the same time, the company began communicating with its auto insurance customers who were heading to the Persian Gulf, suggesting they downgrade their coverage until they returned home. If one spouse from a two-car couple was assigned to the Gulf, the company dropped the rates to reflect that only one person would be driving. The company also told its members not to worry if their payments were late because they suddenly found themselves in a combat zone—their policies would not be canceled while they were away.

As it turned out, Operation Desert Storm—a modern, "Nintendo" war of smart bombs, cruise missiles, night-vision scopes, and computer-controlled tank warfare—generated relatively few casualties for the good guys. All told, USAA paid just $800,000 in insurance claims as a result of the war—not much more than a rounding error in the company's overall financial statements. But it had been prepared to go the whole distance for its members. As McDermott said, in his cut-to-the-chase style, "We insured astronauts—the guys who went to the moon. I figured we'd be strong enough to handle war claims."

Even today, as business executives in a variety of industries around the globe are beginning to embrace the principles of 1to1 marketing, one can only marvel at the foresight and vision of a man like Robert McDermott.

May the Force be with you.

Company: Southern New England Telephone
(NEW HAVEN, CONNECTICUT)

Pioneer: *Patrice Listfield, president, Information and Entertainment Services division*

Lesson: *Corporate culture, organizational structure, and training are the keys. There can be quick wins, but in the long run there is no shortcut in terms of making the transition to a one-to-one enterprise. It will be hard work.*

The CEO of a major manufacturing company declares that his firm needs to become "customer-driven." He issues this directive without explaining how the process of transformation will affect the firm's existing business strategy. He sets a deadline but offers no timetable for implementation. He provides no list of expected outcomes, goals or metrics. He doesn't say who is responsible for leading the effort.

Reacting to the CEO's edict, the firm's most energetic managers devise a series of high-profile customer-focused projects. But the projects have no clear relationship to the company's overall business strategy and there is no shared understanding of their purpose. Not surprisingly, the projects die soon afterward and the phrase "customer-driven" quickly becomes a joke throughout the organization. Demoralized managers seek refuge in traditional product-centered routines, resulting in the steady erosion of the company's profits. A year later the CEO is trying to figure out why the company's best customers have defected to various competitors.

Can this scenario be avoided? A good example of the

right way to handle change can be found at Southern New England Telephone (SNET) in Connecticut, where top management recognized the need to deconstruct the company's rigid vertical hierarchy and replace it with a flatter, more integrated organizational structure. Long before anyone at SNET began drawing charts and tables, top management began "selling" the idea of change throughout the organization.

"First we had to get everybody to buy into the vision that the integration of all our products and services was going to be our competitive edge," recalls Patrice Listfield, president of SNET's Information and Entertainment Services division. "We boiled it down to a fundamental question: Do you believe that being a single-source provider of communications, information and entertainment has value in the marketplace?"

After the fundamental question had been articulated and communicated to everyone in the company, it wasn't difficult to reach a consensus. But that was only the beginning of the process, says Listfield. "After we agreed on the vision, the next question was, How the heck do you get there? There was tremendous debate, and to be honest, we're *still* debating. It's a big and complicated issue. But we had to start somewhere."

For SNET, that "somewhere" was a new organization that replaced the company's stand-alone business units with a matrix of interrelated customer and product groups. After a few false starts, the matrix settled into what SNET calls the "ICEBOX." ICE stands for information, communication and entertainment. The box part refers to the two-by-two matrix of services and customer groups.

SNET "ICEBOX" Customer-Product Matrix

	Consumer and Small Business Group	Custom/General Business Group
Wireline & Wireless (Communication)		
Information & Entertainment		

The ICEBOX concept was simple and straightforward. It was also consistent with the fundamental idea of approaching customers with an integrated palette of services. In retrospect, Listfield says, SNET could have easily chosen any one of several transformational paths.

"We began by changing the organizational structure. Maybe we should have begun by dealing with customer issues, process issues, or system issues and let the organizational issues follow. On the other hand, the benefit of our approach was that it was very dramatic and made a strong statement. Our approach, in effect, said, 'This is where the train is going, decide whether or not you want to get on.' So the message was very clear."

SWIFT VICTORIES

Listfield focused first on achieving some short-term "quick wins," in order to generate support for the concept and build momentum for the changes being made. The first such victory was the consolidation of SNET's in-state and out-of-state toll call services. "It had always made sense to sell them together as one product, but our old structure of separate business units had stood in the way. The new organizational structure made it easy. So now we have one group marketing what we call 'all distance,' a natural grouping of similar products. That was really our first win."

Encouraged by this early success, SNET followed up by bundling its Internet service with the newly created all distance product. "It became another success story and reinforced the feeling that we were moving ahead in the right direction, that our approach made sense, and that our vision was grounded in reality."

Reality, indeed, played a major role in achieving these short-term victories. In both examples, SNET moved to resolve a specific issue that today's telecom customers find especially annoying, namely, multiple vendors and the proliferation of bills that follow. And in both examples the company's actions also served to fend off competition, at least temporarily, from larger telcos with their eyes on SNET's lucrative customer base. "The marketplace defined our response," says Listfield. "What we were doing seemed natural and we went with it."

The quick wins also helped validate SNET's decision to begin its transformation with a series of cautious steps. "When you are describing the big vision, you have to be clear, strong and dramatic. When you get down to changing the way people actually behave, you have to be realistic and move incrementally. This transformation is going to take a couple of years. We're changing the way everybody thinks."

Any multi-division firm such as SNET (which is now a subsidiary of SBC Communications Inc.) faces immense problems in terms of taking a customer-facing view across more than one division at a time, particularly when the divisions are selling to overlapping customer bases through multiple, sometimes conflicting channels.

To visualize the magnitude of the issue, just consider the different customer-facing views of a single business customer taken by SNET's Yellow Pages business unit and its land lines business unit. A very large, very valuable Yellow Pages customer may buy hundreds of thousands of dollars' worth of full-page ads in multiple books each year. But the firm may operate without a call center, and with a series of "retail" phone lines that make it a relatively minor player in the scheme of things, from the land lines perspective. So when such a major Yellow Pages customer has a problem in the land lines area, what does the firm do? How do the land lines folks (a) figure out and (b) act on the fact that this relatively "minor" land lines customer is in fact a very major enterprise customer for SNET?

Or consider the issue of very large business customers whose decision makers are also, for instance, cell phone consumers. Is it in SNET's interest to know that it is having a cell phone billing dispute with a customer who also controls a very large call center budget? Who plays traffic cop here? Who resolves the disputes that will inevitably crop up between different business units serving the needs of the same customers across various divisional boundaries?

Faced with issues such as these, Listfield took the prudent step of enlisting a change management expert to help guide the evolutionary process. Former IBM manager Barbara Brown supervises the day-to-day details of the transformation, making sure that vision and reality don't come unglued. Like General McDermott, she is a firm believer in the value of training and internal communication to reinforce the positive message of change.

For example, as the company weaned itself from the comfortable traditions of a command-and-control environment, it became apparent that not all managers had the skill and temperament required to lead cross-functional teams. So Brown arranged for managers across the ICEBOX to work together on specific business problems, identifying how their roles as leaders needed to change. Engagements such as these served two purposes: They helped prepare the managers for their new roles and reinforced the message that something important was taking place.

Bringing managers together for training also had an unanticipated benefit: It gave the managers a chance to discuss the challenges they shared. For example, managers who thought they were the only ones struggling to maintain a balance between product and customer issues soon discovered that all their colleagues were wrestling with the same problem. Realizing that *everyone* was in the same boat made it easier to begin sharing ideas and solutions that would move the process of change forward.

SHADES OF GRAY

While Brown worked in the trenches, Listfield continued to champion the central message. Listfield's willingness to explain—and re-explain—the purpose of the ongoing transformation became a critical factor in keeping up the momentum, says Brown. "She can effectively communicate the complexity of what we're trying to accomplish. That's not easy. People are very sensitive to mixed messages, but sometimes you can't avoid them. Patrice can make people feel comfortable even when the answer isn't black or white."

Drawing on the growing body of expertise in change management is not a bad idea for anyone contemplating the complex and difficult task of turning their organization toward customer relationship management. David De Long is a researcher and consultant based in Concord, Massachusetts. An adjunct professor at Boston University's School of Management and a longtime observer of change management issues, he dispenses blunt advice to managers who suddenly find themselves under orders to "become more customer-focused."

"Customer-centric initiatives are no different than other broad, all-encompassing change initiatives. If they are too grand, they will usually fail," says De Long. "So make sure the initial effort is tightly focused and linked to business outcomes."

Take care, however, not to expect the parameters of success established in one project to apply in every context or culture. "A dangerous assumption in customer relationship management is that successful projects can simply be rolled out to the rest of the organization," says De Long. "A surprising degree of customer knowledge is embedded in social context, so customer-focused activities—especially in today's global economy—must be adaptable for local practice."

It's easy to see that 1to1 marketing resists the kind of predictable routine offered by traditional strategies. The whole point of one-to-one marketing is that it constantly adapts and evolves to meet the changing needs of living, breathing customers. As long as there are customers out there, the one-to-one manager must scramble to keep up. Continuous change is the staple of this manager's diet, along with a strong dose of ambiguity. Or as Listfield says, "You need to be comfortable with shades of gray."

Companies that "expect everything to be very black or very white are going to have problems," she says. This caveat is worth remembering. As one-to-one programs take hold and spread through an organization, there likely will be pressure to reduce labor costs by standardizing some customer-related tasks that are deemed "routine," such as order taking or certain types of outbound calls.

This kind of pressure should be expected and it's up to the one-to-one manager to devise a response that's both proper and logical. Finding a balance between the urge to standardize and the need to evolve will be a "standard" 1to1 management skill in the future, says De Long.

"Early adopters of one-to-one marketing strategies often find that ongoing adjustments are needed," he says, citing the example of a successful Internet-based grocery retailer whose workers were demoralized by the harsh e-mails they would receive from customers when orders were not 100 percent accurate. To counter the frustrations felt by employees—who were delivering thousands of "perfect" orders every day—management began distributing a weekly summary of key performance indicators that gave the workers a more balanced picture of the grocer's performance.

"Today's communication technologies make it much easier to complain. I'm not saying this is bad, but managers should be aware of the potential impact on employee morale. The lesson is that being customer-centered doesn't automatically mean all interactions will be warm and fuzzy."

Managing the transition means you have to be comfortable with various shades of gray.

Thought Generator
Organization, Culture and Change

At USAA, customer contact is seamless and transparent—as a customer, you see only one company. How many companies do *your* customers see when they interact with your organization? Don't forget that every time you force a customer to repeat information she's already given to you, the relationship between you and the customer goes back to square one. (And she might as well have started over with a competitor.)

General McDermott's successful makeover of the corporate culture at USAA would not have been possible without his personal leadership. He truly believed in his vision of a customer-focused enterprise, and he *sold* that vision throughout the organization. Is a CRM initiative high on the list of corporate objectives at your organization? If so, who is selling the concept within your organization? Is someone responsible for getting buy-in from all levels of staff, in all different departments and divisions?

Patrice Listfield discovered that selling change in an organization like SNET is much easier if you can post some early victories. Can you think of some "quick wins" that can help you to sell the concept of change throughout your organization?

Please e-mail responses to
organization@1to1.com

4

Customer Focus

At most companies there are still very clear organizational boundaries separating the functions of marketing, sales, account management, customer service and production (or service delivery). Marketing sets a brand strategy and develops collateral materials, brochures, promotions, letters, advertising and PR campaigns. Salespeople acquire new business. Account managers make sure that what is sold actually reaches the customer. Customer service handles inquiries and complaints. Production and service delivery render up the product or service that the customer buys.

This system, in which business functions are divided neatly into separate areas of responsibility, has both benefits and drawbacks. On the positive side, it allows people to concentrate on doing what they do best without interference from other departments. It is a straightforward application of Adam Smith's "division of labor" principles to the customer-facing side of a business.

On the downside, however, this type of organization makes it difficult—if not downright impossible—for the company to integrate its treatment of a single customer across different functional areas and business units. It discourages horizontal communication and networking, while promoting wasteful rivalries within the company. It hinders cross-selling and other Share of Customer initiatives.

Still, this kind of separation is fine as long as all you want to do is sell to *markets*. The big problems don't arise until you begin trying to sell to individual *customers*—customers who most likely deal with you across a variety of functions and divisions.

No matter what pretty words you use to define your market (segment, niche, slice, target, whatever), the moment you begin selling into any kind of a market, the clock starts ticking. It's only a matter of time until market pressures will compel you to drop your price to stay competitive. Seeking greater efficiency, you may even be driven to cut corners on quality. And the more successful your product is, the more quickly it will be imitated and reduced to commodity status.

But there is a remedy for this disease. It is 1to1 marketing—focusing on individual customers, one at a time. By remembering your interactions with customers and refining them into richer, more complex and more valuable relationships, you can escape the commoditization trap. The problem, of course, is your organization's structure. If you aren't organized to track customers across business units and functions, remembering their needs and interests as you learn them, then it will be very hard to develop rational, meaningful relationships.

Company: La Mansión del Rio Hotel
(SAN ANTONIO, TEXAS)

Pioneer: *Patrick J. Kennedy, owner*

Lesson: *Motivating employees to note individual customer tastes and preferences is not difficult, provided they are given the tools to do so and they see the fruits of their labor in terms of increased customer satisfaction.*

The 350 employees at La Mansión del Rio Hotel in San Antonio are trained observers. And they are sharp. If a guest arrives and there are golf clubs in the trunk of his car, the parking valet will jot a quick note on a special form he always carries. Then he'll drop the form into a collection box, and by the next morning the hotel's general manager will have personally asked the guest if he needs any assistance scheduling a round of golf at one of the local courses.

When guests revisit the hotel's restaurant, Las Canarias, the waiters will ask if they still prefer the wine they had the last time they dined there. Repeat guests can expect the staff to remember if they prefer a firm or a soft bed, down or hypoallergenic pillows, river or courtyard views. With a unique mix of discretion and vigilance, the staff captures customer data on the fly, first writing it down and then entering it into a database where it can be analyzed and put to use in customer-focused initiatives throughout the hotel.

La Mansión has initiated a program of identifying guests having a special celebration at the hotel. Whether it is an anniversary, birthday or other event, this information is highlighted for the staff, and these guests are provided special recognition, such as an upgraded romantic room and a surprise dessert presentation while dining at Las Canarias.

"Our guests really appreciate this," says Patrick Kennedy, who built La Mansión on the site of a nineteenth-century private school in 1968. "And the results have been impressive. The number of our repeat guests has increased 55 percent in the last two years. And the average revenue per stay of those guests increased 15 percent in the last year alone. Not only did 1998's net operating profit exceed 1997's by 20 percent, but we also beat our 1998 projections by 6 percent. So far, the first two months of 1999 are 12 percent over projections. These techniques really work."

A soft-spoken Texas lawyer, Kennedy is a passionate customer advocate in an industry that has been surprisingly slow to move from product-focused to customer-focused marketing. It's not inaccurate to say that most hotels maintain two distinct lines of products and services, one line for groups and another line for individuals. From a marketing standpoint, the two lines rarely intersect.

"Traditionally in the hotel business, the sales and marketing director is focused on the group market. Very little energy is spent on the transient business. Every hotel knows the walk-in business exists and every hotel is happy to have it, but very few hotels focus on the individual customer," Kennedy says. This shortsightedness makes it exceedingly difficult to boost profits, since group packages are typically discounted to broaden their appeal. Individual customers, on the other hand, offer far greater potential for increased profits—when they are treated as individuals.

In the local market, which reflects a mix of 80 percent group business and 20 percent transient business, La Mansión—because of its intense focus on relationship marketing—enjoys a market mix of 50 percent group business and 50 percent transient business.

At La Mansión, the director of relationship marketing is responsible for growing the transient business, building relationships that will translate into repeat business and managing individual customers. This director reports to the hotel's general manager, who is responsible for making sure that all members of the staff are properly trained and motivated to participate in the relationship-building process.

"Every employee in the hotel needs to recognize that relationship building is a major goal," says Kennedy. "So far, we've found that the employees really like this approach. It elevates the value of what they do, both from a management perspective and from their own perspective. They feel great about it, they feel like they're part of a special team."

The staff understands that, if a guest comments on the beauty of downtown San Antonio, the next logical step is to make sure the guest is made aware of tours or appealing destinations with a strong local flavor. "Obviously, we can't be too intrusive, we have to be subtle and discreet," says Kennedy. "But we want the guests to know that we are trying to add to their experience, to make it more enjoyable and more memorable."

Communicating with as many of the hotel's customers as possible and taking action based on the information obtained is a continuous challenge, says Kennedy. To keep the process from slowing down, he formed a Customer Advisory Council composed of experienced meeting planners and individual guests who have begun holding regular meetings and who are providing valuable customer feedback and enthusiastic support for La Mansión's commitment to improve its personalized guest services continuously.

And La Mansión's management is making changes at the hotel in direct response to customer feedback. For example, the hotel built a business center that incorporated the services and equipment recommended by its guests. Specific menu changes were made in the restaurants to accommodate guest requests and the hotel staff now logs guest-specific allergies into the guest history database.

Kennedy can reel off his reasons for focusing on customer retention:

- The cost of attracting new customers is substantially higher than retaining existing customers.
- A 5 percent increase in repeat business results in a 25 percent or higher increase in profit.

- The "best guests" in a hotel will outspend others by a ratio of five to one.

For the moment, Kennedy defines his "best guests" as anyone who has stayed at the hotel three or more times. "That's not to say we don't treat everyone as special, but our best guests have clearly demonstrated their loyalty to us and so we're clearly going to demonstrate our loyalty to them. A 'best guest' will get a room with a view of the river, rather than the courtyard. A 'best guest' will get the last available room, even if that means we don't rent the room. Guests who return five or more times will get free upgrades to a larger suite, monogrammed bathrobes, or complimentary dinners—something substantially more meaningful than a basket of fruit," says Kennedy.

Kennedy's initiative at La Mansión, and the lessons he has learned during the transformation of the hotel into a one-to-one enterprise, are not that different from General McDermott's earlier experiences at USAA. Both found technology indispensable for achieving dramatic improvements in customer service and customer loyalty, and both paid close attention to the way that technology was integrated into the culture and organization at their firms. Moreover, as pillars of the San Antonio business community, Kennedy and McDermott are professional acquaintances and mutual admirers.

Kennedy is now leading a worldwide campaign to standardize some of the techniques he pioneered at La Mansión. A few years ago, he founded Guest Information Network, Inc. (Guestnet), a company that develops and markets database software designed specifically for hotels. The next generation of the software, scheduled for release in 2000, is an Internet-based system that gives subscribers a robust set of preference tracking tools. It allows subscribing hotels to retrieve, from a central database, preference information on guests who are coming to their hotels for the first time, and gives them expanded data mining and marketing tools that help them craft one-to-one marketing programs for "best guests" across the globe.

"Software, while a critical component in relationship marketing, is just a tool," says Kennedy. "The real challenge lies in changing deeply entrenched hotel culture and the real skill lies in executing consistently over time." And so Kennedy founded La Mansión Hospitality Management Company in late 1998 to develop and market hotel management and marketing services. The management company helps other hotels increase their profitability through cultural change, customer retention, employee development and nontraditional products and services (such as providing personal trainers, nutritionists, beauty consultants, massage therapists or stress management experts) for guests.

Kennedy's long-term goal is nothing short of reinventing the hotel industry as a one-to-one business. "It's an exciting idea—and it's something we have to do. All over the world, the people running hotels are running into the same problems. But they are compelled to worry about short-term issues, such as making their budget. Hopefully, our software and services will give them the insight to make some good decisions. Because if the rest of the world moves ahead with relationship marketing and the hotel business stays where it is today—well, the customers just won't stand for it."

Company: Royal Bank of Canada
(TORONTO, CANADA)

Pioneer: Anne Lockie
Lesson: Technology is critical, but it's not the only thing. In a service business, you need to focus on individual, human interactions with each individual customer. Go where the customer *is. Take the* customer's *interests to heart. Build a relationship based on trust and mutual respect.*

When Charlie, a Royal Bank of Canada customer, swiped his debit card at the grocery checkout counter, the situation quickly became every shopper's nightmare.

Charlie was the kind of customer that every bank dreams of having. He had a big and steady salary, a spotless credit record and probably a million or more in stock options. He was clearly good for the $50 purchase he wanted to make at the local grocery store. But some money had been transferred in and out of his account, and at that particular moment, there weren't enough funds in the account to cover the transaction. So he was declined.

"I mean, somewhere our system should have said, 'Wait a second, this is a high-value client, he's good for the money, let's not embarrass him as he checks out of a grocery store with $50 worth of groceries,'" says Anne Lockie, a senior vice-president at Royal Bank. This is exactly the type of decision Lockie says a small-town banker would have been able to make, back in the days when bankers knew their customers personally.

This is also the type of relationship that Royal Bank of Canada wants to establish with each of its 9 million retail customers. Royal Bank will need to use technology to facilitate such relationships, but in addition Lockie wants to ensure, as much as possible, the same kind of face-to-face service that a small-town banker would have given to his customer. Her goal is simply to make sure that the next time a customer like Charlie gets into this kind of situation, the bank will treat him more like the customer he really is, and less like an anonymous, isolated transaction in a long, precisely defined line of similar transactions.

As luck would have it, Charlie knew a senior executive at Royal Bank and passed on his experience. So, when his request for $50 in grocery money was declined, the episode served as a wake-up call for the bank, dramatically underscoring the importance of developing rational, individual relationships with customers, one customer at a time. Lockie is struggling to move Royal Bank away from its traditional focus on products and individual transactions, and toward a new focus, on long-term customer relationships—relationships that build over time and allow the bank to address the individual needs of individual customers.

The transformation of Royal Bank of Canada will have two distinct and complementary aspects—personal contact with customers, and the technology that will make such contact productive and truly personalized.

Clearly, with millions of customers to relate to, no "personal" relationships would be possible for Royal Bank without technology. The bank will require high-capacity computers and large, highly capable databases to process and store the immense volume of information it has on millions of individual customers. And it will need sophisticated statistical programs, to analyze and understand the implications of this information, and to decide on and test the specific actions it should take with respect to specific customers. Only then can the individual branch managers, account managers, personal bankers, sales executives and even the tellers at the bank be empowered to carry out these actions, with personal contact and attention to individual customers.

There are several ongoing elements of Royal Bank's overall analysis effort. For example, it is now developing and refining the prototype for an algorithm to model the long-term Lifetime Values of its individual customers. As a part of that effort, the bank has also developed a model of "client potential"—a set of statistical equations and mathematical relationships that can estimate how "growable" certain kinds of customers are to the bank. How valuable *might* this customer be to the bank, eventually? What is a client's true potential to do business?

In addition, the bank has done a significant amount of analysis to understand the vulnerability of various types of customers to attrition. If a predictive model could be derived to "flag" the most vulnerable customers at least somewhat in advance of their actual departure from the bank's franchise, then preventive action can be taken in a more focused, effective manner.

Still another set of statistical predictive models is being devised to enable the bank to estimate the likelihood that any particular customer will use additional services offered by the bank. Royal Bank hopes that, by analyzing its data carefully, it will be better able to foretell what products and services its customers might want, and when they would want them.

These efforts have begun to pay off for the bank, not only in better customer relations, but in measurably increased sales as well, when compared to control groups. For example, the bank easily quantified the benefits of statistical analysis in selling its retirement savings plan program. Five different predictive models were used to analyze transactional and third-party information about prospective customers for this program. That information was then collapsed into lists for the bank staff people who would be contacting prospects. The contact list for every staff person was prioritized according to highest opportunities for successful sales, with the prospects ranked and scored to indicate their likelihood of contributing to the program.

The statistical analysis and predictive modeling were applied not just to the customers who had a retirement plan with the bank, but also to identify those customers who didn't—but fit a profile indicating a high propensity to buy into one. Over three months, approximately 1.2 million customers who had plans were contacted, along with an additional 750,000 who didn't. Eight different offers were developed, each one targeted to specific customer needs.

The result? As is frequently the case with this kind of

program, Royal Bank declines to disclose specific figures. But according to Shauneen Bruder, the bank's senior vice-president for marketing and planning, using these models meant the bank had one of its best seasons ever.

In addition, the bank discovered it could grow its most promising customers into even more valuable relationships just by contacting them, even if no specific new product or service were sold to them as a result of the specific contact. "One of the most important things we found," Bruder says, "was that we could lift contributions and penetration rates by up to 10 percent by virtue of the contact alone."

To capitalize on this newly found technological "brainpower" with respect to its individual customers, Lockie knew that the bank must translate its analysis into a form the service and customer contact people could use on a daily basis. She knew the bank would not be able to avoid Charlie's situation without giving line personnel not only more contact with individual customers but the tools with which to understand the true picture of each individual customer.

The intent, says Lockie, is to create on a large and consistent scale the kind of 1to1 relationships that come naturally to small-town bankers working in the community alongside their customers. Obviously, with such a large customer base and the advanced technology needed to analyze customer patterns, it would be tempting for Royal Bank to focus on the quantity rather than the quality of those individual relationships. However, all of the company's research and anecdotal evidence says that customers *want* to be treated as more than just numbers.

They want to be treated as individual people by individual people.

"The more people deal with us electronically, the more difficult it is for us to generate that kind of relationship with an individual customer," says Lockie. "That's why, with our one-to-one strategy, we need to make people feel they're genuinely connected with us, and that we actually do know them, personally. . . . We can now get to our customers with the right offer at the right time. And, for us, the key value proposition involves customizing our offers to customers in a one-to-one fashion. In fact, all our marketing programs are called 'one-to-one.' But then it's a question of prioritizing our scarcest resource—the time and energy of our front line sales staff—so we can spend more of our effort simply contacting the right customers."

So, on one level the bank aggressively deploys its analyses of customers and customer types, equipping sales and service people with detailed customer profiles. By arming its people with such analytical information, the bank can safely empower them to make a variety of on-the-spot decisions, based on individual customer value, rather than simply carrying out a one-size-fits-all policy.

But on a second level the bank also encourages its employees to get out of their offices and onto the customer's turf. The results are sometimes highly creative. For example, there is a banker who works in a dairy barn. He's what's called a "mobile banker."

Most of the bank's mobile bankers work out of their homes. Each one has a truck, a cell phone, and a laptop. They take care of the bank's larger farm clients. "So they go to the people's farms and sit down one-to-one with them and understand what they are doing," Lockie says.

This particular banker was not able to work from home, but he had a lot of clients who were dairy farmers. "There's an auction barn where a lot of the dairy people come in and out," Lockie explains. "So our guy made an arrangement with them to rent an office there and work out of it. Basically, he took our laptop and cell phone and worked out of our office, using the barn as his base of operations."

Lockie says the solution represents a good example of how the bank tries to allow its employees to create a working situation that enables them to interact more frequently and more effectively with their customers.

Note that for Royal Bank of Canada, a financial services organization, the process of tailoring its relationships with individual customers necessarily involves a flexible and innovative approach to service employees, as well. "The relationship we're trying to develop with each individual customer is going to be different. It was a short step for us to translate the same thinking into our employee care initiatives. Because we also know that every employee is different," Lockie says. "We've started down that road so that people can begin to customize their own benefits package, select their own insurance and so forth. People can now decide for themselves. And it's also up to them when they work and from where.

"In Saskatchewan, about 10 percent of our sales force works from home, or they work out of someplace that makes sense for them," Lockie says. "I have mortgage reps working out of real estate offices. I have the guy working out of the dairy auction barn. They go and work and set up shop where it makes sense for their clients. So it works for our customers, but it also works for our employees."

This not only helps the bank's staff to develop one-to-one relationships, Lockie says, it also helps them meet other customer needs as they come up, further cementing the relationship.

"The added value for us is not in the products we sell anymore. Because these products you can buy anywhere, off the shelf. They are all the same. A financial product is a financial product. The only value added really for the clients is advice," she says. "And what we more and more are becoming is purveyors of advice."

However, because talking about and sharing information about finances is considered a taboo in Canadian culture, the bank must also make certain that its many terabytes of customer data remain private and securely protected.

The bank has to make every effort to assure customers that its employees are treating their private financial information with respect. Again, we face the issue of trust. And at Royal Bank the executives understand that trust will become a bigger and more important issue as more and more sensitive data are collected about customers.

"We have done some groundbreaking research into what privacy means for Canadians," says Bruder. The research shows that Canadians are more sensitive about privacy, when it comes to financial matters, than their American counterparts.

Lockie and her colleagues know that privacy issues

have to be tackled up front. "We have to be proactive with Canadians in telling them about privacy and how to deal with it in this new electronic world. Then we have to make commitments to clients about how and what we will do with their own personal information. And we have to let them know that, at the end of the day, they own that information," says Lockie.

"We've just done a new privacy video, and we have a number of privacy materials that we can provide to customers and other folks who are interested. Our objective is not just to be able to describe our privacy codes quickly and simply. What we're also trying to do is to use our privacy expertise and privacy-protection policy for competitive advantage."

Developing and institutionalizing privacy issues at the bank is yet another way for the bank to make sure its staff is practicing another good, old-fashioned banker's attribute: discretion.

Lockie knows that continuing along this path is critically important. The bank *must* use technology to understand its individual customers, and then it *must* put its line personnel in front of these customers, individually, to carry a more personal relationship directly to each customer.

And if they didn't do this? If they were to write off the "Charlie incident" and simply stick to selling the transactions and products they know so well?

"We'd be out of business," says Lockie. "And it wouldn't take long. The competition is getting so severe that it's just impossible to compete in any way other than this way."

Company: Oxford Health Plans
(NORWALK, CONNECTICUT)

Pioneer: *Steve Wiggins, founder*

Lesson: *Automation and technology must be used not only to treat customers better but to take care of the most basic business functions, too. If you grow your business fast, be sure you grow your information technology capabilities just as fast.*

Remember how the sorcerer's apprentice became intoxicated with his newfound magical powers? Automation can have a similar effect, especially if it leads managers to overestimate the capabilities of their organizations. Steve Wiggins, the brilliant entrepreneur who created Oxford Health Plans in a spare bedroom and grew it within a few years into a multibillion-dollar managed care giant, knows this danger better than any man alive. "We had mud on our windshield and we couldn't see reality," he says, reflecting upon the computer problems that beset his company just as the managed care industry was experiencing its first real shakeout. "We got hit the hardest because we were the fastest-growing."

For example, problems with the information system made it impossible to price commercial group policies accurately. At the same time, Oxford was blindsided by Washington's decision to slash Medicare reimbursements during the push for a balanced federal budget. Unfortunately, the government's drive to economize coincided with steeply rising medical costs for Medicare patients.

Oxford's slow but steady recovery from a shock that

would have shattered most corporations reveals the durability of relationship-based marketing strategies. Months of negative press, scoldings from various regulatory agencies and a score of shareholder lawsuits had little effect on Oxford's membership rolls. Even when the company curtailed services and raised premiums, the customers stayed loyal.

Although Oxford's financial problems forced Wiggins to step down from the CEO post, he remains one of the company's biggest fans. He isn't surprised that Oxford has held on to its members. "One of the reasons we were rated so highly in customer satisfaction polls was that people feel we care about them. They feel they have a real relationship with us."

Oxford nurtured these relationships in several ways. Staffing and resources were allocated to retention marketing programs that utilized member information in ways that inspired trust and reinforced the core message. Programs such as Active Partner, Healthy Mother/Healthy Baby, Healthy Bonus and Alternative Medicine were designed to create tighter bonds between the members and the company. Programs such as these represent the epitome of relationship marketing initiatives:

Active Partner reminds members about the importance of key preventive care measures such as mammograms and Pap smears. Members who have missed important tests are identified through an analysis of claims data, based on age and gender. Women over age fifty, for example, are reminded to schedule an annual mammogram if the database indicates they haven't already done so. Women over eighteen are reminded to have Pap smears. Diabetic members are sent reminders for retinal eye exams. Reminders explaining the importance of early immunization are sent to parents when their children are eighteen months old. Members over sixty-five are encouraged to get a flu shot during the winter season. Teen-age and adult members are reminded to schedule annual checkups.

Healthy Mother/Healthy Baby is designed to identify and manage high-risk pregnancies, increase the rate of full-term pregnancies, reduce the rate of low-birthweight babies and encourage healthy behaviors. Pregnant members are sent educational materials on an array of topics including prenatal care, exercise during pregnancy and nutrition for mother and baby. Because expectant mothers have many questions, Oxford set up a toll-free prenatal help line staffed by specially trained maternity nurses who answer questions and offer advice. If a mother-to-be requires extra guidance and care during pregnancy, an experienced maternity case manager is assigned to work directly with the member and her OB/GYN to help solve problems and provide a reassuring point of contact.

Healthy Bonus provides discounts on products and services that can help members achieve their health or fitness goals. For example, seniors are offered an exclusive fitness program. Parents of small children are offered discounts on car seats, bike seats and bike helmets.

Alternative Medicine is an effort to accommodate the willingness of Baby Boomers to seek out nontraditional approaches to healing and pain relief. Oxford set up a credentialed network of alternative care providers including acupuncturists, chiropractors, naturopaths, message therapists, nutritionists and yoga instructors.

Wiggins made sure that all new members got a phone call after joining the health plan. "We'd call up and ask them if they'd gotten their membership cards," says Wiggins. By giving the company a human voice, those simple calls played a key role in Oxford's early success. Not only that, but tests using a control group showed that the simple act of receiving a phone call significantly improved a member's likelihood of renewing with Oxford at the end of the plan period.

Wiggins had the advantage of starting with a clean slate when he began Oxford. There was no "institutional memory" to contend with, no entrenched bureaucracy to fight change, no pre-existing circumstances. Instead, Wiggins ran the company as if it were an ongoing experiment. Every member was a partner in a continuous process of invention. Heavy customer contact was seen as essential, because each contact offered the chance for a new idea to germinate. "My view was that we were manufacturing our product at that moment, at that nanosecond," says Wiggins.

Fueled by an unusual mix of entrepreneurial genius and utopian idealism, Wiggins rapidly built a world-class, customer-friendly health plan. Membership increased dramatically, driving annual revenues from $100 million to $4 billion in just six years.

Throughout these years of phenomenal growth, Wiggins stuck to his customer-friendly philosophy. On the surface, it still resembled a one-to-one approach. At frequent employee meetings Wiggins reinforced his philosophy of treating each member differently. He sent company-wide e-mail and voice mail messages to announce new programs. He became a daily presence on the company intranet site, where he had a page called "Steve's World."

But there was a dangerous shortcoming in Oxford's overall business growth plan. You can't grow a company at a rate of more than 100 percent a year for six years without dramatically scaling up your information technology capabilities—especially if your whole business model is predicated on providing immediate access to individual customer information. Oxford's computer systems never actually seemed to catch up with the company's growth rate and information needs. In 1997, a growing chorus of resentment was being heard from physicians and other providers who justifiably claimed that Oxford wasn't paying them on time. This was because Oxford's financial systems were collapsing under the weight of the firm's expansion.

When Wall Street suddenly got wind of the problem the stock plummeted spectacularly, losing more than half its value in a single trading day, perhaps because investors feared that Oxford must have a vast amount of underreported liabilities to physicians. But the truth was, Oxford just couldn't tell who was owed what, because its systems were in chaos. It wasn't billing its employer customers on time either.

That Oxford survived and appears to be heading back

into good financial health is a direct result of the customer-friendly habits that remain deeply embedded in the company's culture.

Company: French Rags
(LOS ANGELES, CALIFORNIA)

Pioneer: Brenda French, owner

Lesson: Necessity may sometimes be the mother of a one-to-one marketing business model, but the desire to please customers is a one-to-one marketer's single biggest reason for being.

Custom knitting comes naturally to Brenda French. She learned when she was a little girl in northern England. Like many people of her generation, she had no choice. During World War II and the harsh years that followed, stylish clothing was a luxury. If your family wasn't wealthy, the only way to obtain stylish clothes was to make them yourself.

Born of necessity, French's talent for creating remarkable fashions evolved into her life's passion. She spent years learning the trade as a freelance designer in New York. Then in 1978, divorced and the sole provider for her young son, she launched the company that would become French Rags. Her first products were colorful scarves, knitted at home and sold to friends for little more than her basic costs. Within months, word of mouth excited such demand for her scarves that she began selling them to major retailers and specialty stores including

Lord & Taylor, Neiman-Marcus, Bloomingdale's, Robinson's and Ann Taylor. Soon she had a factory in Los Angeles and had expanded her line to include sweaters, jackets, skirts, blouses and accessories. From 1978 to 1989 her sales skyrocketed from $168,000 to $8 million.

Then a series of bankruptcies and cash crunches hobbled department stores across the United States. French was forced to cut off stores that couldn't pay their bills. As her distribution channels shrank, annual revenue plunged to $1 million and French began shipping product C.O.D.

That's when her customers rode to the rescue. A prosperous East Coast fan offered French the use of her home to sell clothes directly to other admirers who wanted to stay loyal but could no longer find French's fashions on retail shelves. French threw her collection into a few trunks and headed east, hoping to unload maybe $10,000 worth of merchandise. The visit succeeded beyond her wildest expectations. Not only did she sell what she'd brought, she took orders from women for clothing she promised to make as soon as she returned to L.A.

French wound up grossing $80,000 from the trip, enough cash to start up her business again. It also permanently changed the way she looked at doing business. Why deal with intermediaries, she figured, if you can sell direct to your customers? The girl who had kept knitting during the Blitzkrieg put together a new business model and relaunched French Rags as a direct-to-consumer manufacturer of high-end, mass-customized knitwear. Because the clothing is high-quality rayon knit, it can be

folded without fear of creasing. French Rags are especially favored by women who travel frequently and don't
want the hassle of carrying a separate garment bag for
dressy clothes.

Today, from a digitized factory floor in a former motion picture studio on Tennessee Avenue in Los Angeles,
French Rags creates 30,000 individual items per year—
each custom-made for a specific client. Four times annually, a new collection, usually composed of 300 basic de-
signs available in a choice of 60 custom colors, is shipped
to a small army of 100 sales consultants across the nation,
drawn from the ranks of her satisfied customers. Indeed,
French's customers and consultants form a virtually seamless network of interlocking social circles, exchanging un-
filtered information with the logical efficiency of a
complex natural organism.

The consultants hold trunk shows, often at their homes,
to display French's latest collections. Customers are beck-
oned to these shows with one-of-a-kind, hand-illustrated
invitations that double as collectibles. Meetings between
consultants and customers are by appointment only, im-
parting a certain sense of purpose to each encounter.
Women don't arrive at these appointments to shop—they
arrive to buy. It's not uncommon for a single appointment
to generate several thousand dollars in sales.

On average, the consultants book 40 to 60 appoint-
ments for each collection. Samples are shown, measurements taken and colors chosen. Orders are written up by
hand and faxed to the home office. French plans to auto-
mate the system at some point in the future, but for the

present her consultants are comfortable working with pen and paper. And in this company's culture, comfort is considered indispensable.

When French decided to open a permanent showroom in Los Angeles, she rejected a standard boutique setting for it. "I had a bit of an epiphany," she recalls. "I suddenly realized that one reason we do so well is because we sell in people's houses." So French hired an architect, dug up part of the factory parking lot and built an actual "house," complete with living room, dining room, kitchen and bathroom. There's even a little garden to complete the homespun image. "It's a myth that women love shopping," French says. "All this 'shop till you drop' stuff is passé. On the other hand, women still want to look terrific and they still love clothes. So the question is how to make buying easy and enjoyable."

The customers are blissfully unaware of the novelty and originality of French Rags's business model. But then, why should they be concerned with it? The customers simply feel as though they are pampered, looked after and cared for. They are, and it's hard to tell what came first—the business model or Brenda French's passion for forging a palpable, deep-rooted emotional bond with her customers. "I'll tell you something funny," French says. "A psychic once told me that I have programmed into me this incredible need to make women happy. I really do get a big kick out of it. I love dressing women, I love taking care of them and I love making them feel good. Women come up to me, give me a big hug and say, 'You've made my life better.' For me, that's a real turn-on. It makes me feel like I'm doing something important."

But the simple fact is that—in sharp contrast to almost all other consumer manufacturing businesses everywhere—a French Rags product doesn't even exist at the moment of its sale. And, unless alterations are required, the finished goods are very seldom returned. In the custom clothing niche, of course, returns can wreak havoc on profits, since they're impossible to resell at anything near full price. In a very real sense, therefore, French Rags lives or dies on its ability to deliver continuous customer satisfaction.

Delivering continuous customer satisfaction, in fact, pretty much sums up the thrust of the French Rags operation. When pressed, French will tell you the real reason she's in the business is because she loves making other women look great. She'll say the reason she and her crew work long, hard hours producing fashionable knits is because their customers are part of an extended family they are eager to please. Remember: they're not producing clothing for some anonymous shelf in a shopping mall outlet. At French Rags, each article of clothing being manufactured is destined for a specific individual's wardrobe. Every item, in effect, "has a customer's name on it" from its very inception. In French's factory (or "craftory," as she occasionally calls it), manufacturing is a conscious act of high-tech alchemy that turns a conversation between two women into a piece of fashionable apparel.

Sales consultants at French Rags can tap into a deep base of knowledge about each individual customer's tastes and buying preferences. They are encouraged to show styles they think their customers will actually buy, based on this knowledge. To add to this knowledge, French

Rags offers its customers a "closet audit" program. Using an off-the-shelf digital camera and specialized software from Atlanta-based ImageWare Technologies, the sales consultant creates a digital, visual record of each item in her customer's wardrobe. Having such detailed records at her fingertips gives the consultant an incredible selling advantage. Not only does she know what her customers already have, she can predict with reasonable certainty what they will need next.

For example, suppose a customer were to fall head over heels for a new fall jacket. In this case the consultant, who would have studied the customer's closet audit prior to meeting with her, would remind the customer that she doesn't have pants to accompany the new jacket and might suggest a couple of new pairs to go with it.

The sales consultant is acting as her customer's trusted agent, a role only made possible because at the heart of French's business strategy is the need—the *desire*—to deliver continuous customer satisfaction.

Company: Carrollton Fire Department
(CARROLLTON, TEXAS)

Pioneer: Bruce Varner, fire chief

Lesson: Yes, 1to1 marketing and basic customer service principles can easily be applied to government services. Indeed, because most governmental agencies don't engage in these "customer-friendly" practices, it is all the more remarkable when one does.

A wonderful example of a basic service surrounded with an envelope of personalized care can be found in Carrollton, Texas, where the local fire chief has trained his firefighters to be customer-conscious and user-friendly. In this case, the "customers" are town officials who control the fire department's budget. The end-users are homeowners and apartment dwellers who dial 911 when a fire or medical emergency occurs. Why do Carrollton firefighters go out of their way to build trusting relationships with the people they serve? Isn't it enough to show up and put out the fire?

Let's take a closer look. In most communities, including Carrollton, fire fighting is regarded as a standard public service. You count on it being there when you need it. While the flames are raging, nobody cares whether a firefighter is polite, sensitive or caring. The only two things that count are saving lives and limiting destruction. But what happens *after* the blaze is another matter, says Fire Chief Bruce Varner.

"The aftermath of a fire has a tremendous impact on a person," Varner notes. Even when there are no physical injuries, the emotional trauma can be intense. Someone whose house has just burned down is likely to be confused and disoriented by the experience. That's when a special level of care and understanding is needed. At the moment when most fire departments begin packing up their gear, Varner's firefighters morph themselves from smoke eaters into service reps.

After a fire, a fire officer takes the time to walk homeowners or tenants through the charred wreckage. He explains the extent of the damage. He assigns firefighters to search for valuables, such as wallets, books or jewelry boxes, that might be hidden under piles of rubble. He offers the use of a cell phone and guidance on finding temporary shelter. He'll even find a safe place to park the family car.

To Varner, each fire call represents an opportunity to build a relationship that will come in handy when the municipal budget is under review. He knows that small acts of kindness go a long way. For example, if firefighters see a deep freezer full of shell steaks in the basement of a burned-out home, they will run an extension line to a neighbor's house so the meat won't spoil. If a business is involved, they will help protect its stock from further damage. Recently, when a family-run business risked losing its inventory of Beanie Babies after a fire, Varner called up his counterpart at the sanitation department and asked him to send over some clean barrels to serve as temporary housing for the stuffed collectibles.

This carefully nurtured culture of service hasn't gone unnoticed: The people of Carrollton rate their fire department as the top service organization in town. In the rough-and-tumble world of local politics, that kind of good feeling is a powerful defense against the bean counters at town hall.

Thought Generator
Customer Focus

While perhaps not as dramatic as the problems faced by customers of the Carrollton Fire Department, your own customer relationships will be subject to occasional crises. Can you predict the likely crisis points—events that will pose traumatic threats or difficulties for your own customers?

If it becomes necessary, could your organization help customers through these crisis periods, in "above and beyond" ways that would tend to increase your perceived value to the customer?

Good customer service is not always synonymous with 1to1 marketing, which is based on individual customer relationships. In what ways do you think the Carrollton Fire Department simply provides good customer service, and in what ways is their service customized to individuals? What might they do to generate even better one-to-one relationships?

How does your organization measure customer attrition? How about share of customer? Can you—like Royal Bank of Canada—build predictive models that define which customers to keep and which ones to grow?

At La Mansión del Rio, Patrick Kennedy has calculated that a 5 percent increase in repeat business translates into a 25 percent increase in profits. Can you calculate what a 5 percent increase in repeat business would do for your own bottom line? With that number in mind, how would you start generating more repeat business using 1to1 principles?

French Rags builds to order, as opposed to building to market forecast, so their in-channel carrying costs are virtually zero. Could your organization do this? Which of your customers would be happiest with this? What are the incremental steps between where you are today and a build-to-order model? Which of these steps are technology- and process-based, and which are people-based?

Oxford Health survived a potentially fatal blow for one reason: Their customers stayed loyal. Could you depend on customer loyalty to survive such a crisis? What could you do to increase your chances?

Please e-mail responses to
customerfocus@1to1.com

Culture of Service

A fter a series of odd twists and unusual turns, Western society has embraced a new economic aesthetic, one that basically says it's often better to *do* something cool than to *own* something cool. Why *buy* a new car when you can *lease* it? Why *invest* in a lawn mower when you can *contract* with a landscaping service? Why *accumulate* things when you can just as easily *borrow* them?

Business has mirrored this phenomenon, reversing the questions while preserving the intent. Why manufacture products (high costs, low margins, little flexibility) when you can sell intangible services (lower costs, higher margins, unlimited flexibility)? Why incur huge capital expenses when you can invest your money more wisely in software and human resources?

Again, of course, technology plays a role. It is technology that permits a firm to reconfigure its service to meet the needs of individual customers, and to do so cost-efficiently. Because of technology, a manufacturing company no longer has to limit itself to producing a single-size product and trying to find a larger and larger number of customers for it. Instead, by thinking of its business in terms of the problem it is solving for its customers rather than the product it is selling to them, the firm can cultivate service-based *relationships* with customers.

Or, as Pitney Bowes's president, Marc Breslawsky, puts it: "Why build fax machines ourselves when we can hire some other company to build them to our specifications?" And while Pitney Bowes sells more fax machines than anyone else, Breslawsky will tell you quite candidly that he's in the messaging business, not the fax business. His customers don't really even want fax machines—they just want their messaging needs handled, and that's what Pitney Bowes is focusing on.

You can argue about which came first—the service economy or the service mentality—but it's a chicken-and-egg question. Any company—even a manufacturer—focused on relationships with individual customers must concentrate on the problems it is solving for its customers, rather than the customers it is finding for its product. Think about it: If you make something to order, is that really manufacturing? Or aren't you really now in the service business?

Service, in the old-fashioned sense of the word, involves an unwavering focus on individual customer needs. Service with a smile. The customer is always right. It is this kind of service that is now returning to the forefront of business competition. Why? Because technology is making it possible once again.

Company: Pitney Bowes
(STAMFORD, CONNECTICUT)

Pioneer: Marc Breslawsky, president
Lesson: Concentrate on solving the customer's problem, not on selling your own product. Products come and go. It's the customer relationship that will last.

Welcome to the new mailroom. It may sit on your hard drive. It may be on your server. It may be somewhere "out there," on the Internet. Even if your mailroom is still an actual, physical room not too far from the loading dock, chances are that at least part of it exists in cyberspace. As more and more digital packages join the ever-increasing stream of cardboard and paper packages, the mailroom has evolved into an entirely new animal. Few companies are more aware of this than Pitney Bowes, which built a franchise around the postage meter.

"The mailing business used to be very mechanical," recalls Marc Breslawsky, president and chief operating officer of Pitney Bowes. "But the needs of our customers have changed greatly over the past few years. So today you find that most mailing products involve software. That's the only way you can deal with the variety and complexity of needs out there. Let's say you're a big utility, for example. You need to send out invoices, but all your customers don't necessarily want to get them by standard mail. Some customers will want their invoices faxed directly to them. Others will want to get their invoices via e-mail. Some might want to access their invoices over the Internet. It's likely that some might want to pick and choose among several channels. The point is, you've got to be able to accommodate their needs."

To a far greater extent than ever before, Pitney Bowes is called on to explain this phenomenon of expanding customer needs to its clients, some of whom are clearly surprised by the sudden complexity of new demands and rising expectations. "When they're not aware of these needs, we sit down and work with them. We try to see which of these new customer needs might create new values for our client. One of these needs could be the basis for a tremendous new product," says Breslawsky.

One could argue that "product development" at Pitney Bowes has evolved into something very different. Call it "specification development" for lack of a better phrase. Working closely with its customers, Pitney Bowes creates specifications for hardware and software that will meet their actual needs. Some products are developed and manufactured by Pitney Bowes, others are developed and produced by OEMs, original equipment manufacturers. It's fair to describe the fax machines and copiers marketed by the company as the physical manifestations of carefully cultivated customer relationships.

For example, a few years ago a large automotive company approached Pitney Bowes with a problem: Many of its employees travel extensively or work frequently from remote locations. These employees needed a way to pick up faxes sent by customers while they were out of the office. The obvious solution—call the customer from whom you're expecting a fax and give him your temporary fax number—was considered too customer-unfriendly. Pitney Bowes assigned its engineers to write a custom software program that let the automaker's employees dial into their office fax machines and download documents that had been sent to them while they were on the road. Security and privacy were maintained by establishing a system of personal mailboxes to hold the incoming faxes. The enabling software, which began as a custom feature, is now standard on all Pitney Bowes fax machines.

Breslawsky is convinced that this culture of service has become his company's primary competitive differentiator. "None of these customized services could be described as a price point purchase. Every one of these activities is a value added to the client. If they pay us X for a customized service, they are going to make $X + Y$ *percent* on it. It's the same with the fax machines and copiers. They're built to specs developed with the customer in mind and designed to create value for the customer by enhancing that customer's productivity."

Creating an atmosphere in which customer needs take center stage wasn't an overnight process. For decades, everyone knew Pitney Bowes as the company that made postage meters. Durable, dependable, consistent and predictable, these devices were the workhorses of every corporate mailroom. The company's direct sales force had no problem finding homes for each postage meter that rolled off the assembly line. In the mid-1980s, new management set more aggressive goals. Growth rates would have to be accelerated dramatically, new products would have to join the established line-up and the sales force would need to refocus on selling applications and intangibles such as value-added services. As early as 1992, the company's former chairman, George Harvey, had begun planning for a future in which traditional mail was no longer the "default mode" for sending written messages. Long before the term "killer app" entered the popular lexicon, Harvey foresaw that fax, e-mail and voice mail would someday rival surface mail as the corporate world's preferred system of messaging.

Harvey was from the old school of corporate management—buttoned-down, exquisitely polite and socially conscious. But he wasn't shy about sharing his hard-edged vision of a future in which postage meters no longer played a solo role. This set the stage for the radical transformations that would come over the next few years. "We needed to go through a major cultural change," says Breslawsky. The philosophy of the status quo—come to work, do your job, go home—was replaced with a philosophy of personal responsibility that made everyone in the company accountable for customer satisfaction. "We asked ourselves: Who in this company is responsible for customer satisfaction? Is it the salesperson? Is it the service person? Is it the billing person? Is it the collections person? Is it me?

"The answer we came up with is this: *Anyone who touches the customer is responsible for customer satisfaction.* We can do a great job selling and we can do a great job servicing, but if a customer calls in with a question about an invoice and the person who answers the phone comes across as uncaring or rude, then everything else we've done is lost. So we tried to develop an attitude in the company that we are totally customer-driven and that everyone who works here is responsible for customer satisfaction. This represented a very significant cultural revolution that took place over three or four years. A lot of our employees had their doubts. Some were very willing to continue living with the old culture, even though it was becoming obvious that this culture wasn't helpful to our customers."

This service culture is illustrated vividly by the company's disaster recovery service, which sets up a sort of "virtual mailroom" to cope with major emergencies. The capability evolved from a series of responses to customer needs. It began with an understanding that the "speed of business" had changed.

For example, some of the company's larger clients rely on machines capable of producing millions of mailings per month. If the machine stops for even a few hours, it could delay tens of thousands of pieces of mail. If those pieces of mail happen to be bills, the impact on revenues can be substantial. In the past, customers would grin and bear it when their mailing machines broke down in the middle of the night. But that sort of tolerance has all but evaporated in today's faster-paced economy. So Pitney Bowes asked its larger customers if they were interested in signing up for round-the-clock repair service.

Next the company began providing specialized training so clients would be able to restart their own machines, reducing downtime from hours to minutes.

"Then we took it to the next logical step: We asked

them if they would like us to run the equipment for them. In other words, *don't just buy the machine, buy the capability,*" says Breslawsky.

Following this path, Pitney Bowes developed a full-fledged, off-site disaster recovery service. In case of power outages or other emergencies, clients can download all their information to the computers at Pitney Bowes. "We'll do everything from here. We'll do the printing, the inserting and the mailing. You wouldn't know the difference between something produced at your site from something produced at our site," Breslawsky says.

So far, the evolutionary process seems to be on track. The company has posted fifteen consecutive quarters of earnings growth and more than doubled its market cap—from $7 billion to $15 billion—in the past two years. Most of the people who were working at Pitney Bowes *before* the company shifted its focus from products to customers are still there. "I think we've succeeded in a much shorter period of time than many other companies," Breslawsky says with understandable relief. But in his competitive gut, he knows the race is far from over.

Company: General Electric
(FAIRFIELD, CONNECTICUT)

Pioneers: Richard Costello, corporate marketing communications manager; Klaus Huber, European sales director, Aircraft Engines division

Lesson: One-to-one marketing programs work at many levels. By recognizing that the bundle of services sur-

rounding a product—such as a jet aircraft engine—can be more profitable than the product itself, companies can boost margins while building customer loyalty.

When you hear the words "General Electric," chances are you think of light bulbs, refrigerators and NBC. One of the world's largest corporations, operating across dozens of industry sectors, GE is feared by its many smaller competitors as a numbers-driven Goliath. The image isn't entirely unwarranted. But there's considerably more here than meets the eye. In its business-to-business lines—which now represent the largest chunk of GE's total sales—GE strives to achieve the same level of customer intimacy as First USA Bank or French Rags. What's fascinating is that GE's push toward customer focus is developing the greatest momentum in business lines not traditionally associated with "intimacy."

"Our most complex and intimate relationships develop in our large capital goods businesses—jet engines, medical systems and locomotives," explains Richard Costello, GE's corporate marketing communications manager. In these situations, initial purchase prices range from millions of dollars to hundreds of millions of dollars. Despite these intoxicating numbers—just imagining the commissions is enough to make you dizzy—GE encourages its executives to look beyond initial sales and consider the long-term value of customer retention to the company's bottom line. "We've realized that our ongoing relationship with the customer is just as important as the original purchase if not more so," says Costello.

Although GE probably won't be auditing your wardrobe in the near future, its jet engine businesses regularly perform what could be called "wing audits" to determine the exact needs of their airline customers. From GE's point of view, the relatively small number of customers—there are only about 300 airlines in the world—makes the monitoring process highly manageable. Additionally, the purchasing cycles of these customers are usually well known. So it's not difficult to project sales revenue with reasonable certainty. What's less easy to foresee, however, is the strategic value, or what we call Lifetime Value, of this customer base. This is where things get interesting.

You can't just bolt a jet engine to a wing and forget about it. For the sake of both safety and economy—and also because it's legally required by the FAA—you've got to maintain that engine in superb condition. Jet engines are subject to continuous maintenance. Over its lifetime, a jet engine will be torn down and rebuilt many, many times. From the customer's point of view, the expense of maintaining a jet engine is far more significant than its initial purchase price. The vendor has a similar perspective—it's far more profitable to *maintain* a jet engine than it is to *sell* a jet engine. So much more profitable, in fact, that most jet engines are steeply discounted, sometimes to the point of being sold at cost. It's fair to say that jet engine makers and airlines have evolved relationships that resemble marriages. There's simply no such thing as a short-term relationship between a customer and a vendor in this sector. Breaking off the relationship poses serious consequences for both parties. "So our key objective is to make the relationship between us and the customer as painless and as seamless as possible," says Costello.

To accomplish this, GE has launched a do-or-die effort to develop high-value extranets for its large capital goods customers. Anyone who buys a GE jet engine now knows that mission-critical information is a mouse click away. The latest FAA directives, as well as any safety bulletins, are posted on a special extranet designed exclusively for jet engine customers. Blueprints, wiring diagrams, modifications and schematics—the contents of eight to ten volumes' worth of printed material—can be accessed from the extranet site. In some cases engine problems can be diagnosed in flight with the aid of sensors capable of beaming real-time performance data to service personnel on the ground. Spare parts can be ordered over this private network, which also allows customers to monitor shipping status. This feature alone saves airlines tens of thousands of dollars, since it enables them to make decisions based on real-time knowledge instead of hunches and intuition.

For example, if a 747's EFIS (electronic flight information system) malfunctions while it's on the runway in Djakarta, the airline can choose intelligently between shipping a new component or sending another plane all the way to Indonesia to pick up the stranded passengers. A quick trip to the extranet will make it clear if the component is available, which warehouse it's sitting in and how long it will take to get it to Djakarta. The extranet, says Costello, "is not only a competitive advantage for us, it's also an incredible tool for building customer loyalty." In a very real sense, GE is blurring the distinction between the physical product and the information surrounding it. It's as if marketing were playing by the rules of quantum physics, where it's often difficult to distinguish between matter and energy.

Similar extranets have been designed for customers of GE's medical systems business. Here again, the goal has been to leverage the power of a Web-based platform to surround a tangible product with an envelope of high-value information.

"The companies we compete against also offer highly advanced technologies. It's tough for us to get a sustainable competitive advantage in terms of product alone. So we're looking to develop advantages in the service and the information surrounding the product," says Costello. GE can remotely track the operational status of its medical systems worldwide, twenty-four hours a day. An imaging device in a Boston hospital will be monitored during the day by GE technicians in Milwaukee. When the Milwaukee team's shift is over, it hands off to a team in Tokyo. Eight hours later a team based in Paris takes over. When its shift is through, Milwaukee picks up the ball again.

"Smart sensors will alert the technicians to any variance in the machine's operation. Based on the machine's known performance characteristics, the technician will diagnose and troubleshoot the problem. In most cases, we are able to alert the operators at the hospital before they even notice something's out of kilter. And if necessary, we will dispatch technicians to the scene to fix the problem *before the customer has even asked for help.* This is what we mean when we say we're using information to build intimate relationships with our customers and this is where it will be tougher for the competition to match us."

More and more, Costello says, the company is finding that its customers are seeking relationships, not products. The best example of this trend can be observed in GE's locomotive business, which now sells "power by the hour"—a service that essentially guarantees freight delivery by rail. Service offerings such as these tacitly acknowledge the obvious, namely, that someone who buys a locomotive is interested in moving freight from Point A to Point B. The engine is only a means to an end.

"This represents a big cultural shift for us," says Costello. "In the old days, the salespeople were trained to act like elephant hunters. They'd go out on the game hunt, find a big customer and bring back a half-billion-dollar order. Nowadays, for example, the pricing on jet engines is so brutal that they're sold at cost or worse. So the money has to be made in parts and service. As a result, we have these large service operations around the world that we didn't have a decade ago. And the people leading those operations have changed too. Even as recently as five years ago they were basically wrench-turning guys. Not high-profile types, certainly not the leading management people in the company. Now we've shifted some of our top talent into these service operations. We want to focus our resources on these service operations because they've become very valuable profit centers for us. Our Aircraft Engine Services division is now as important a business as our jet engine equipment manufacturing operation."

Klaus Huber, director of European sales for GE's Aircraft Engines division, doesn't mince words when talking about the role of 1to1 relationships in building long-term profitability. "What happens *after* they buy your product—is everything. In this business, you can't leave people in the lurch. Because they'll never come back to you again."

Lufthansa is Huber's largest account. While his German ancestry certainly helps him win friends in the Lufthansa hierarchy, Huber's success as a manager is based on his ability to maintain a steady stream of communication between GE and the airline. A small squad of GE technicians and engineers assigned to the Lufthansa maintenance shop provides "elbow-to-elbow" contact with the client. While this "live-in" arrangement guarantees daily exchanges between the jet engine maker and its end-users, it's only part of the relationship process. In addition, Huber manages the overall relationship with the help of a formal entity called the customer team, or CT. The CT is composed of representatives from various specialties such as sales, customer support, technical services, parts and repair. "All of us talk together on the phone every day. We make sure everybody on the team knows what the customer's needs are. We make sure we're servicing those needs. And we look for new opportunities to serve the customer."

Although conversations among team members are kept informal—nothing kills creativity faster than forcing people to fill out forms, Huber says with the rueful smile of someone who's been there, done that—they are a granular component of a much larger, structured effort launched back in 1995 by GE chairman Jack Welch. With the same sense of now-or-never urgency that marked his earlier campaign to flatten GE's table of organization, Welch embraced Six Sigma, a program designed to reduce defects and assure quality. (Imagine a bell curve measuring standard deviation. Three Sigma would represent about 50,000 defects per million operations. Six Sigma would be less than 4 defects per million—practically zero.) Although Six Sigma was initially devised to address product quality issues, the program now reaches into practically every corner of GE. For Huber, it means taking his customer team on a trip to Hamburg to interview Lufthansa managers. The interview process, called a QFD (quality field deployment), generates a list of CTQ (critical to quality) issues. Working together, the GE customer team and the customer prioritize the list. This puts both sides in synch, greatly reducing wasted exertion. As Huber puts it: "If we're working on a problem like crazy but it's not a problem Lufthansa cares about, then why are we working on it?"

The prioritized CTQ issues are then mapped onto a "customer dashboard"—a chart complete with illustrated dials and gauges that show precisely where the team stands in terms of satisfying the customer's needs. "Not only are there numbers on the gauges, they change in color from red to yellow to green. We work hard to keep them in the green. If you can take a customer's problem and solve it crisply and quickly—they'll love you forever."

Over the years, customer-driven behaviors have played a major role in the success of the Aircraft Engines division. During the 1940s and 1950s, GE provided aircraft engines solely to the military. In the 1960s the company saw an opportunity to sell into the commercial aviation market and differentiated itself largely by establishing a more customer-friendly environment than its competitors. Today GE is the leading provider of the jet engines used on wide-body aircraft—the most lucrative part of the commercial market.

Huber embodies an interesting synthesis of Welch's concept of the "boundaryless" organization and our vision of the fully integrated, one-to-one enterprise in which "turf wars" are obsolete and mission-critical information flows seamlessly across divisions. "When a problem happens, we don't argue about who's at fault," says Huber. "If the plane isn't flying, our customer is losing money. We know the clock is ticking, so we go in and fix it, no argument. Responsiveness is our game."

Huber recently improvised a quick fix for a client in Luxembourg with a malfunctioning jet engine, rounding up a spare engine from GE's leasing operation. From a strictly contractual standpoint, the client's problem should have been handled by GE's customer support function. "But I'm the guy who sold them the engine. So I got on the phone and found out leasing had an engine available in Rome. We got the engine ready, they flew down to Rome, picked it up, flew it back to Luxembourg and put it on the wing. Technically, I'm just the sales guy. But I will run against any barriers to keep a customer's airplanes flying."

Company: SAS Institute
(CARY, NORTH CAROLINA)

Pioneer: Dr. Jim Goodnight, CEO
Lesson: Culture matters. If you want great relationships with your customers, it helps to have a great corporate culture—and one that rewards excellent customer service.

Dr. Jim Goodnight. It's a catchy name, but not one most people would instantly recognize. Dr. Goodnight is cofounder, CEO and president of SAS Institute—the world's largest privately held software company. He is a tall, laconic man with close-cropped hair and the eyes of a hunter. Colleagues aptly describe him as resembling a mature John Wayne cast in the role of a statistics professor. Goodnight began his career by writing complicated programs that analyzed farm statistics. He learned programming in the early 1960s, when he was a student at North Carolina State University. Back then, each line of code required a separate punch card. Programming was slow, tedious, lonely work. Goodnight remembers the school's computer. "It was small. Only one person at a time could use it. I would go over in the middle of the night and try to make my programs work. What fascinated me was the Selectric typewriter that would type by itself. That was the computer's only output device. It was just so amazing."

The days of click-clacking Selectrics and punch cards ("Do not fold, bend, spindle or mutilate") are long gone. But the sense of amazement lingers. In the past two decades Goodnight has seen data processing migrate from mainframes to mini-computers, to PCs and back to mainframes, which now are often used as servers. In each migration, SAS managed to stay ahead of the trend. This ability to perceive impending change and react before the market has been a primary factor in the company's success—twenty-two consecutive years of double-digit revenue growth; 17,000 customers representing more than 3.5 million end-users sitting in front of screens at 31,000 sites in 120 different countries and 5,400 employees working in 50 nations around the world.

Dr. Goodnight's "secret weapon" is the company's unwavering commitment to developing customer relationships that result in a continuous flow of information between the company, its clients and end-users. Most of the firm's new products, in fact, are developed with the direct involvement of one or more customers. "There's no reason to develop products customers don't want," Goodnight says. Not that SAS hasn't tried, he adds. "A few years ago we had some three-dimensional animation technology. It looked pretty exciting and so we made a large investment in it. After we had developed the product, we discovered there really wasn't much of a market for it. You do that a few times and you learn to listen to your customers—and do precisely what they want."

This isn't just talk. Goodnight's philosophy has been carefully institutionalized in a variety of programs and organizational structures designed to support a customer-centric approach to business. For example, the company mails an annual SASware Ballot to customers and end-users. The ballot is a compendium of suggestions for new software features, a "wish list" of options, add-ons and capabilities. Customers and users vote for their favorites.

The ballot serves as a sort of virtual thermometer, taking the temperature of the company's customer base at regular intervals. It also provides SAS with a detailed, timely snapshot of customer needs. Results of the balloting are forwarded to the company's research and development division, which implements more than 85 percent of the input. Results of the balloting also are discussed at user group conferences hosted by SAS. The conferences, held throughout the year in locations around the world, provide an opportunity for SAS users to meet face to face with SAS product developers, guaranteeing fresh and unpredictable exchanges of ideas and information. Goodnight credits the conferences with generating the serendipitous flashes of insight that led SAS to begin writing software for mini-computers and, later on, for PCs. In both instances, SAS customers had seen the wave coming from a distance: By listening to them, SAS caught the wave at precisely the right moment.

Goodnight and three fellow programmers incorporated SAS in 1976. It specialized in providing unsexy but indispensable programming tools for collecting and analyzing huge amounts of raw data. SAS itself is an acronym for Statistical Analysis Software, which tells you exactly where Goodnight and his colleagues were coming from. The tools were sold to large customers whose programmers then used them to develop their own solutions. This model worked fine as long as the universe of customers was limited to companies with "heavy iron" mainframes. With eerie prescience, SAS began developing Multivendor Architecture in the mid-1980s. This architecture freed SAS from the forced burden of making either/or choices between operating systems when developing new programs. "We didn't have to change 100 percent of our code as we went from machine to machine. Instead we had a host layer that acted as a virtual operating system. So we only had to rewrite about 10 percent of our code for each platform. It's similar to what you see happening today with languages such as Java. We were probably twelve years ahead of that concept."

Over the next few years, mini-computers began replacing mainframes in many areas. Then the PC came along and universalized computer use. Suddenly the demand for software outstripped the availability of programmers. Goodnight saw the emergence of an entirely new class of customers—business executives who were comfortable using desktop computers and who needed a wide range of software solutions but had absolutely no desire (or time or expertise) to write their own programs. For SAS, the message was obvious: The company would have to expand its array of software products to remain competitive. Now the question was: What will these new products be? Goodnight's reply: Ask the customers and end-users. "We've *always* been customer-driven. The products we develop are based on what our users ask for. We have *always* relied on the customer to tell us what to do. It's our nature. This is not something *new* for us."

It would be easy to dismiss these protests as New Age posturing if the evidence didn't weigh so heavily in Goodnight's favor. It's hard to find an aspect of life at

SAS that isn't permeated by Goodnight's customer-centric philosophy. SAS staffs its marketing groups with customer relations specialists whose primary mission is maintaining open dialogues with customers about SAS products and services. Using a Web-based interface, these specialists relay detailed feedback from customers to marketing, sales, service, R&D, corporate communications and other relevant divisions within the organization. Customer data are shared globally via CARD (Customer Application Reference Database), greatly enhancing its value. Real-time numbers showing the exact dollar amount of revenue generated by each customer are available online to the SAS workforce through the company's Customer Information Warehouse.

"Global access to information gives everyone at SAS the big picture for each customer. For example, an account executive who is planning to initiate new activity with a customer can check to see if that customer has any outstanding software issues," says Goodnight. By looking closely at how customers are currently using their software, SAS consultants can determine whether integration issues are looming. Technical support reps can scan the database to see if someone else in the organization has already solved a particularly thorny problem. Success stories are posted on the company's intranet so they can be shared across the organization. SAS even sends video production crews to some customer sites to document how its software is being used.

To ensure that customer information *never just sits but is always working,* SAS reaches into its own portfolio of products. SAS uses Enterprise Miner, an industrial-strength data mining tool with a graphical user interface, to explore its customer database, discovering any underlying trends, needs or relationships that might have gone unnoticed. "We're so fortunate that we have enough customers so we can actually do this kind of analysis," says Goodnight. (Imagine, for a moment, the sheer thrill of drilling through a customer database that contains 98 of the Fortune 100 companies!)

SAS recently formed a new division to develop products based on the specific needs of customers. Marketers, consultants and developers were culled from their respective divisions and relocated to Building A—a building with historical significance because it was the first structure erected on the sprawling SAS Institute campus in Cary, North Carolina. The new group, called the Business Solutions Division, initially operated as a company within the company, sort of a "skunkworks" where new ideas could flourish. Its goal was to draw upon the organization's formidable expertise in data warehousing, data analysis and reporting to create enterprise software packages that would address common, everyday business problems. Several new SAS products, including HR Vision and CFO Vision, emerged from this effort.

HAPPY WORKERS, HAPPY CUSTOMERS

It would be impossible and possibly even misleading to discuss SAS without mentioning its unusual devotion to keeping its employees happy. *Fortune* ranks SAS as third-best company to work for among the nation's top 100 companies. *Working Mother* magazine lists it among the top 10 best companies for working moms. *Business Week* recognized SAS as among the best companies for work and family. Even *Mother Jones* magazine weighed in, listing SAS among the 20 "better" places to work based on parameters such as charitable giving, progressive benefits, sound environmental practices and employee satisfaction.

It's hard to ignore the old-fashioned—some might say medieval—values embedded in the SAS culture. To begin with, the lush 200-acre campus in the rolling hills of North Carolina is exquisitely landscaped—by SAS employees. No outsourcing allowed. Everyone you see on that campus works for the same company, from the top executives to the kitchen crew. There's a 35,000-square-foot indoor fitness facility; neatly manicured athletic fields surrounded by loblolly pines, oaks, maples and sweetgum trees; a well-equipped day-care center and a health clinic. They even have baby seats in the cafeteria. Standard workdays are seven hours. And of course there are the M&Ms. Despite his tough-guy persona, Jim Goodnight is a softie when it comes to sweets. He makes sure that all employees get their fair share of the little candy-coated chocolate spheroids, delivering them by the bushel to each building on campus like clockwork every Wednesday. When asked about his commitment to keeping employees happy, Goodnight is characteristically blunt. "If you've got a revolving door with your employees, it's very difficult to build up long-term customer relationships," says Goodnight, circling back to his core theme. SAS employees receive above-average pay, but few of the trendy compensation perks—such as stock options—associated with the software industry. Nonetheless, the company's turnover rate is less than 5 percent. The industry average is more than 20 percent.

The way Goodnight sees it, employee retention is responsible for the company's high rate of customer retention. Employee retention also translates into more opportunities for building high-value relationships *within* SAS. "One of the things I believe in is that ideas come from the bottom of the organization. The lowest levels of the organization are where the best ideas come from, because that's where they're looking at suggestions and ideas from the users. They'll put together programs based on those ideas to see if they'll work. Then their managers will pass the ideas up to me and if I like it I'll fund it." Goodnight pauses as if explaining something very fundamental to a small child. "I recognize I don't have all the ideas in the world. There's a lot of other people out there with ideas. All I do is sort of let them run with their ideas. That's the way we do things here."

Company: Bell Atlantic
(NEW YORK, NEW YORK)

Pioneer: Doug Mello, president, Large Business Services-North

Lesson: Becoming a customer-focused company does not always require having the latest technologies and Web tools. It can be as simple as focusing on the most old-fashioned of values—trust, confidence, reliability, dress code.

Doug Mello remembers the day Bell Atlantic began its journey toward becoming a customer-focused company. It was February 26, 1993, the day the World Trade Center was bombed.

"That was the big turning point for us. By eight-thirty that morning we had restored telephone service to our 786 customers at the Trade Center. We had our biggest customers, we had our smallest customers—all back in service. We opened up our lobby for the cops and firemen to make calls. We even fed them."

At that crucial moment, Bell Atlantic's public image as just another "fat cat" telco evaporated. Seizing the moment, the company reinvented itself as a good neighbor, a caring member of the community, and—most important—a company that really cared about its customers. Now all it had to do was live up to its new image.

Frankly, that meant change, and plenty of it. Bell Atlantic would have to drastically alter its culture, its organization, and the way it measured success. The old measuring standard—total billed revenue—would be joined by a new metric, one that focused on customer satisfaction.

The company conducts annual face-to-face surveys of its top 300 accounts. "I get paid—and *every* manager in my organization gets paid—on the basis of how well we do on those surveys," says Mello, who serves as president of Bell Atlantic Large Business Services-North.

"The survey interviews can take anywhere from an hour and a half to two hours. This is taken very seriously. The customers are asked what they think of their account manager, their salesperson, the quality of the installation, maintenance, billing—everything. Then we ask them how we compare with MCI, AT&T and others in the field. We ask them what share of their business they're giving us and what share they're giving our competitors," says Mello.

Internally, the staff is required to predict the results of these surveys up to four months in advance, assigning them color codes (green, yellow or red) to assess the current level of satisfaction. "We encourage everyone to be truthful. The goal is to eliminate surprises. If there's a problem, I'd rather fix it sooner than later."

Mello requires his sales force to hold monthly service meetings with their counterparts from operations. This puts service issues front and center. "When there's a problem, I don't call the operations people to find out what's wrong—I call the salesperson," says Mello. "Some of the salespeople don't like this, they say, 'Gee, I'm spending 50 percent of my time on operations issues,' but this has taught us to stay focused on customer service."

Mello's jurisdiction includes two of the most competitive markets in the United States, New York and New England. For many clients, especially those in the financial services sector, anything less than 100 percent uptime is unacceptable. "One of our clients is the New York Clearing House, which processes $1.5 trillion worth of transactions daily. It can't have *any* downtime. None. So I go over their survey with them personally and if they're having a problem, I follow up on it until it's fixed."

This level of management involvement represents a significant departure from the traditional command and control corporate culture. Despite his conservative suits and expensive silk ties, Mello is an agent of change. And yet a significant part of the one-to-one manager's role is figuring out what *doesn't* need to change. As an organization begins shedding behaviors that impede customer-focused programs, some managers will be tempted to change *everything*. Striking a balance between what needs to be *fixed* and what needs to be *left alone* isn't always easy.

Faced with intense pressure from a growing roster of ravenous competitors, Bell Atlantic relies on experienced hands like Mello to steer a course from the past to the future without capsizing.

As Bell Atlantic—or any established company—evolves to keep pace with younger, more agile competitors, it risks alienating some of its clients. Even in the midst of change, however, organizations must take care not to break the bonds of trust that secure customer loyalty. The message to customers that essentially says, "Yes, we're changing, but you will remain our top priority," must come from the top, says Mello.

"My customers still know they are the most important people in my universe," he says. "By word and by deed, I visibly demonstrate this commitment every day. I roll up my sleeves and get personally involved. I make as many customer calls as possible. I visit our branch offices to stay in touch with our account executives, especially the less experienced ones, just to see how they're doing. Running a customer-focused operation is a very hands-on job."

Mello's ability to find the center of gravity and then set the right tone for his staff is not an inherited talent—it's a carefully developed skill. Mello has no illusions about his managerial proficiency—he knows that without constant practice that proficiency would vanish.

"Every two weeks on a Monday morning I get all my branch managers and my vice-presidents together on a conference call that doesn't last more than twenty-five or thirty minutes. Everyone opens up and talks about their biggest service problems, where the backlogs are. I have a method for dealing with problems. I call it 'once around and up.' That means that, if they can't solve it quickly at their level, I expect them to come to me and I'll help them. I'll go right to my opposite number in engineering or operations and say, 'Hey, buddy, I need your help.' That way, we throw everything we've got at the problem and together we make it go away. No standing on ceremony, no running up and down vertical silos."

Customer focus is maintained through the company's Major Customer Service Centers. Employees responsible for servicing the company's 300 largest accounts are grouped into modules to ensure that the same employees stick with the same accounts. "Everyone who touches the account—from the sales rep, to the repair clerk, to the line tester—sits together within the same four walls. They handle that customer together, every day."

For example, the Citibank account has its own module. Chase Manhattan Bank has a module. The City of New York has another. "If I'm going to make a call on Citibank, I'll go right to the Citibank module and find out if there's been any trouble, how the latest installation went, what's the revenue picture, where we are going with the account."

As the marketplace around him changes, Mello prides himself on knowing which old-fashioned values to cherish. He believes in handwritten notes to recognize good work. When he's disappointed, he takes the time to craft a constructive message instead of sending off an angry e-mail. He also spends a lot of time shining his shoes—and making sure his sales force presents an image of rock-solid reliability.

"Not everyone has to wear a Brooks Brothers suit, but I want my staff to look good because it inspires confidence. I once actually installed mirrors in all my branch offices. I told everyone to look in the mirror before they go out on a sales call, make sure they're sending the right message. Believe me, it works. We have clients who stay with us even when our competitors come at them with lower prices. That's because we inspire confidence and trust."

Thought Generator
Culture of Service

New service opportunities can create tremendous sources for both revenue and profit growth from existing customers. How else might Pitney Bowes capitalize on its positioning of being in the "messaging" business?

Can you name a product where you spend more on service than for the initial product? Is the manufacturer selling you the service as well? If not, why not?

At GE, there is an explicit, ongoing effort to increase the value of the company to its customers by blurring the border between product and service, so it all becomes a single, indispensable relationship. What could your firm do to convert individual product sales into such lifetime service-and-information relationships?

What is the biggest single stumbling block to converting your organization into a 1to1 enterprise? If you wanted to follow Marc Breslawsky's lead and "stir up the corporate culture" at your company, what would you do?

SAS Institute customers stay loyal despite aggressive marketing efforts from competitors. How many of your customers would stay loyal if they were offered a better deal by an established competitor? Why would the loyal ones remain?

At most of the organizations mentioned in this book, everyone who comes into contact with a customer is held accountable in some way for customer satisfaction. If this were the policy at your firm, what would the implications be? How would such a "culture of service" impact hiring and promotions? Budgets? ROI and other business plan metrics?

At Bell Atlantic, a portion of executive compensation is specifically allocated to customer satisfaction. What metrics would you use to determine your own customers' satisfaction levels? Could you use such metrics to compare the performance of your own company's executives? (Be careful! Measuring comparative customer satisfaction is trickier than it appears. See *Enterprise One to One*, pp. 116–20.)

Please e-mail responses to
serviceculture@1to1.com

6

Knowing the Customer

Two types of expertise are required for a successful business: product expertise and customer expertise. You have to have product expertise to deliver the best product or service to your market. No matter how good your relationship is with your stockbroker clients, if you don't have reasonably defendable investment recommendations, you're not going to be in business very long.

But customer expertise is one thing many businesses overlook. Knowing a particular customer's preferences is an extremely valuable asset when it comes to getting more of that customer's business in the future. All other things being equal, in fact, the business that has the *most* customer expertise, with respect to a particular customer—the business that knows that customer the best—is more likely to get that customer's business.

Product expertise and customer expertise are both important, but in the long term customer expertise is more defendable as a competitive proposition. You can't prevent your competitors from doing research and acquiring just as much product expertise as you have, at which point your customers will have a choice between two commodity-like products.

But in order for a competitor to develop the same level of *customer* expertise as you, with respect to any particular customer, that customer will first have to interact with your competitor the same way as he has already interacted with you. The more information you develop on any particular customer—by observing the customer's transactions with you or by interacting directly with the customer—the more potential benefit there will be, in terms of maintaining that customer's loyalty.

Knowing your customer means being able to change the way you treat a customer, based on what that customer needs or what the customer is worth. But you can't know your customer without data, a database, and some analytic applications.

And your enterprise can't really "know" your customer at all unless you make this information available at every point within the enterprise that comes into contact with the customer. So having customer knowledge not only means obtaining the data and extracting insight from them, but also communicating the insight within your enterprise. And it means having a system for collecting new information from customers as it becomes available.

Sometimes knowing the customer can be no more complicated or sophisticated than setting up a system to track his or her transactions. Other times, it can require a comprehensive database of your customer's preferences and tastes. Still other times, knowing the customer can mean something as simple as meeting the customer face-to-face.

Company: Dick's Supermarkets
(PLATTEVILLE, WISCONSIN)

Pioneer: *Ken Robb, senior vice-president of marketing*
Lesson: *It's not enough to collect voluminous customer information. The payoff comes from using this information to create customized treatment for individual customers.*

Ken Robb has a secret. Truth is, though, he's not really the secretive type. He's very open, never hesitating to say what's on his mind, which is a good thing, because Robb is senior vice-president of marketing at Dick's Supermarkets, a chain of eight stores in rural Wisconsin. Okay, so it's not exactly like being director of the CIA; the "secret" Robb has isn't likely to interest James Bond. Let's just say Robb is a guy who knows something his competitors don't.

Robb's secret is that he knows pretty much what his customers intend to buy when they go shopping. That, along with a reputation for superior service, is Dick's Supermarkets' primary defense against lower-priced competitors and category killers. DataVantage, a software product developed by Relationship Marketing Group (RMG) of Connecticut, sifts through Robb's scanner data to predict when his customers are likely to repurchase specific products. The system then generates special offers on a "just-in-time" basis.

How it works: Customers who spend $25 or more per week at Dick's are sent a customized shopping list every two weeks. The list is a composite derived from the customer's purchase history and current offers, deals or discounts from manufacturers. Customers can bring their lists with them when they shop or leave them at home. When the customer gets to the register, the clerk scans the list (which is imprinted with a bar code) or the customer's regular Savings Club card. Either way, any special offers on the list are automatically redeemed and the customer's purchase history is updated for the next list.

"It's great for us and great for the manufacturers because you can customize the promotions. You can make an offer that's directly proportional to the value of the customer's business," says Robb.

Dick's Supermarkets also relies on customer-specific information to aim tailored promotions at its most valuable customers across a variety of categories. For example, users of nonaspirin products such as Tylenol could be divided into three groups: national brand, store brand and brand switchers. Within each of those groups, customers could be tiered into three subgroups based on low, moderate or high usage. Usage is a proxy for the customer's long-term value to Dick's, within the category. (In just this one product category, there are six "modules," yielding a total of nine different types of customer—more than enough to drive a mass-customized marketing campaign.)

If the supermarket's goal, for instance, were to convert Tylenol users into store brand users, Robb would save his most aggressive campaign for heavy users because they offer the most potential value. Heavy users would be offered deeper initial discounts than low and moderate users. The promotions would be timed to coincide with each customer's unique buying cycle, which Robb can predict with reasonable accuracy by analyzing the customer's purchase history.

"Customers think it's cool because the shopping list is a reflection of what they buy. If they have a dog or cat, they're getting dog food or cat food offers. If they have a small child, they're getting offers on kid stuff, or diapers and baby food. Someone who buys a lot of vegetables will get a lot of vegetable offers," says Robb. "If they shop at more than one supermarket they miss out on some offers that would have been triggered by their purchase history with us, because obviously we don't know what they're buying someplace else. But if the majority of their business is with us, then typically they're getting a list of fairly significant value. It's not unusual for our better customers to get a list with as much as $35 or $40 worth of coupons. The goal is to reward customers who spend the majority of their food dollars with us."

Sometimes it's possible to minimize the damage that discounting will do to your economics by obtaining funding from other interested parties, in return for sharing the data you're collecting. In the case of Dick's Supermarkets, manufacturers fund most of the discounts. As part of the overall package, the manufacturers get access to a trove of highly detailed sales information (with names stripped out) processed by Relationship Marketing Group, which not only supplies the software but also mines the scanner data.

A quick aside: Be careful here. While frequency marketing and bonus card programs are a great way to collect customer data, they are often misapplied, with self-defeating results. The first tasks for a one-to-one marketer are to *identify* and *differentiate* customers, and so in the retail category a frequency marketing program like the one offered by Dick's Supermarkets can be an indispensable aid. It provides individual customers with the incentive to "hold up their hands" every time they go into the store, to get their discounts. The actual mechanics of a frequency marketing program also provide a great platform for *interacting* with customers, either in the mail, or at the register, or even on the Web.

But here's the danger. Frequency marketing is a tactic for producing individual customer information and interaction, not a strategy sufficient to make customers loyal—not in the face of a similar promotion from a competitor. To turn this information and interaction into a Learning Relationship, ensuring your customers will find it more convenient to stay loyal rather than participating in a similar program offered by your competitor, you have to do what Dick's Supermarkets does. You have to *customize* your treatment of each individual customer, based on the information. Then, as you collect more information about any single customer, your treatment of *that* customer can be tailored more and more specifically, giving the customer a kind of collaborative investment in the service you are giving him. In addition, to the extent possible, such a program should include not only highly tailored discounts but also such nondiscount incentives as recipes, weekly meal plans, tips on product usage, health and nutrition information, expedited checkout lanes and even home delivery services.

Never, never forget that the goal of marketing is *not* to give stuff away.

In the short term, immediately after launching a loyalty program, it's easy to forget this. You might be deceived into thinking that giving stuff away has made your customers more loyal. But when your competitor launches a similar program, and your customers can now get discounts at either store—then what do you do? Who wants a bunch of customers who are always looking for discounts? All you will have done is train your very best customers to look for price breaks.

In a "typical" U.S. city surveyed by ACNielsen in 1997, three principal grocery competitors each had a frequency marketing program. Loyalty program participants accounted for more than 90 percent of each competitor's dollar volume. But three quarters of these participants carried more than one loyalty card in their wallets, and more than half of them carried all three!

So remember what puts Dick's Supermarkets on the short list of good one-to-one marketing practitioners: Robb *uses* the information he obtains from his customers to offer them an incentive his competitors can't easily duplicate, because the incentives are tailored to each customer's individual preferences and purchase cycles. The more a customer shops at Dick's, the more specifically tailored that customer's benefits will be, and the more incentive there will be to remain loyal. This makes it a very hard program to compete against.

Robb thinks of this information as his little secret. "In most situations," he says, "if your competitors want to know your pricing, they come into your store and check the prices on the shelves. Or they look at your weekly ad. But with this shopping list, your competitors have no idea what you're doing, because everybody gets a different list!"

Company: DaimlerChrysler/debis Financial Services (NORWALK, CONNECTICUT)

Pioneer: Stephen Cannon, director of marketing
Lesson: Treating different customers differently can sometimes be such an obvious course of action that it hits you right in the face. When it does, grasp the opportunity and apply it every chance you get.

When the Berlin Wall was demolished, Stephen Cannon had a front-row seat. He was a lieutenant in the U. S. Army, fresh out of West Point, assigned to patrol the East German border. It was a time of uncertainty, excitement and danger. The infamous border would soon vanish, joining the ghosts of history. Germany was reunited. The Soviet Union dissolved. The Cold War ended. Cannon says his vivid memories of those events provide him with a healthy perspective on the demands of corporate life. "When somebody tells me they're going to *die* if something doesn't get done on time, I have to smile. On the other hand, I know why it's important to keep tearing down the walls that separate us."

These days, Cannon tears down walls in the world of high-end specialty leasing and financing. He heads the marketing group at debis Financial Services, a rapidly growing subsidiary of DaimlerChrysler. Before joining debis, Cannon led the marketing effort behind Mercedes-Benz's introduction of its M-Class sport utility vehicle. The M-Class launch presented Mercedes with two daunting challenges. First, very few people in America associated the Mercedes-Benz brand with sport or utility. Second, although these types of vehicles had become popular during the early 1990s, Mercedes-Benz got into the market late and wasn't prepared to unveil a production model until several years later. So Cannon and his team came up with the idea of developing a long lead relationship campaign for prospective M-Class customers. "We knew there was a huge overlap between Mercedes owners and people who owned sport utility vehicles such as the Grand Cherokee, Explorer and Range Rover. We knew we had to get onto their radar screen."

Cannon decided to introduce the car to these potential buyers in the form of a series of "sneak previews" designed to pique interest and elicit feedback while the new car was still in the development stage. The Mercedes-Benz customer database was mined to identify and differentiate potential M-Class customers. "We had a prospect hierarchy. The strongest were Mercedes owners who also owned luxury sport utilities. Next strongest were Mercedes owners who also owned lower-end sport utilities. We sent them reports and updates as the car was coming off the development track in Tunisia or being test-driven through the Alps."

Each mailing had a response form to establish a dialogue between the company and the prospect. With response rates running as high as 65 percent, Cannon knew they had latched onto something. Midway through the campaign, the responses indicated that many prospects thought the car looked small. They thought it looked more like a Honda CRV than a Suburban. "With our next mailing, we sent them a luggage tag. We told them the tag was for all the extra bags you could pack into the M-Class because it's got more luggage space than an Explorer or a Grand Cherokee. We were constantly tailoring the message, based on what we heard, to drive home our point. You listen to the customer, then adapt your message."

The M-Class launch gave Cannon the experience and confidence to apply similar techniques at debis. "No matter where you go, everyone's using the 'R' word—relationship. Especially when you're dealing with a commodity such as money. If you can't build a relationship with the customer, if you can't create a bond—then what's going to hold the customer from going anywhere else to get money? On the car side, you have a wonderful product recognized all over the world. In financial services, the relationship is what you hang your hat on. It's all you've got."

At debis, Cannon's mission is to grow a portfolio of custom loans and leases for big-ticket items such as luxury mega-yachts, high-speed ferry boats, cruise ships, jet aircraft, construction cranes, and even golf courses. In some situations, debis finances both ends of the deal—the construction or fabrication of the product itself and the loan or lease that lets the end-user sail, fly or drive off in it. Developing and maintaining expert knowledge across a variety of industries is another critical piece of the relationship-building puzzle. "Let's say we're financing a construction crane. We've got to understand the seasonal nature of the crane operator's business so we can structure a deal that coincides with his cash flow. In another case, we tailored a deal for a helicopter tour company so they could skip payments in their off season. That's our competitive edge over banks. We develop relationships, we learn about the unique needs of our customer base and tailor our products to meet those needs."

For example, by surveying the habits of customers in the pleasure marine category, debis learned they upgrade with surprising frequency. "They buy a little boat for $500,000 and it's not in the water six months before they see the next bigger boat and they want to buy it. Our customers told us they'd like to see a periodic update on their credit value, so they know exactly how much more boat they can afford. So now we update them periodically. For our best customers, we translated these updates into a personalized, pre-approval program. We timed the mailing of the pre-approval packages to coincide with the Fort Lauderdale boat show, which is the largest boat show in the world. We sent our pre-approved customers a special card with their name on it and their new credit limit. This was important for our customers because it immediately distinguished them on the docks as serious buyers, not just tire kickers out looking for a free tour of a big boat." The initial test of the concept resulted in $11 million worth of new loans—all from existing customers.

Company: British Airways
(JACKSON HEIGHTS, NEW YORK)

Pioneer: Woody Harford, vice-president, business travel marketing USA

Lesson: No matter how good the service is, even if it is absolutely excellent, it's still important to personalize your relationships with your customers. In addition to improving the service, relationships will return measurable financial benefits to the firm.

Woody Harford has a dual identity. On the surface, he's just another executive at British Airways. But swirling beneath the corporate veneer is Harford's other self: *customer champion.* When there's a battle between customer needs and company needs, Harford and his team step in to fight for the customer. "My job is to make sure we are making decisions based on the needs of our customers, rather than basing decisions on what's most convenient or economical for us. That's not to say that I want to deliver the most expensive service. What I want is to deliver services that offer real value to the customer. It's up to us to figure out how to deliver that value at a price that makes sense to everyone."

Harford, whose official title at British Airways is vice-president of business travel marketing USA, isn't bucking the system when he struggles on behalf of the customer. Since the mid-1990s the airline's mantra in the United States has been customer intimacy, shareholder value and people development. All three are inextricably inter-twined, says Harford.

"We all know that our customers are also the custom-ers of our competitors," he says. Indeed, the universe of frequent international business travelers is quite small—somewhere between 150,000 and 250,000 individuals. This relatively small base of customers, however, repre-sents a disproportionately large share of revenue and profit for international airlines. "We share the same cus-tomers, so we need to treat them better than our compet-itors treat them. Believe me, they can tell the difference between airlines."

An early adopter of 1to1 marketing, British Airways understands the significance of identifying not only end-users but also the people who influence each phase of the decision-making process. This is especially true when dealing with small or medium-size businesses.

"Historically, the airline business has been so filled with intermediaries—everything from travel agents to corporate travel departments—that it's very difficult to get your message to the end-user. That's the person we want involved in the decision-making process—the per-son who actually gets on the airplane. But at the same time, we are well aware that in many small or medium-size companies the CEO or the CFO—maybe even the CFO's assistant—might be helping to make the decision. It's a complex circle of influence and we needed a way to relate to everyone involved in the process. So part of our job is identifying all these various people who influence the decision. And naturally, it's a different group of people in every organization, which makes our task all the more difficult.

"So we developed Venture Club, a business-to-business relationship marketing program modeled on frequent flyer programs. Venture Club allows the organization to accrue benefits without affecting an individual's ability to earn personal frequent flyer rewards. There's a designated person within the organization who controls the distribution of those benefits, so they can be used in a way best suited to that organization. The credits then could be used to defray the costs of buying a new state-of-the-art copier. Or office supplies. They could be used to reward employees for good performance. The customer—not British Airways—determines how the benefits are used."

British Airways hopes Venture Club will prove an effective tool for attracting, keeping, and growing small to medium-size firms that can't generate enough volume to qualify for contracted discounts. Ideally, the program will allow the airline's field sales reps to build better (and more profitable) relationships at these firms while simultaneously reducing the pressure to pursue higher-volume deals that would entail heavy discounting.

For individual flyers, Harford is counting on an innovative program to accelerate the pace of cultivating the airline's Most Growable Customers and turning them into Most Valuable Customers. The program uses predictive modeling techniques to maximize revenue opportunities from new customers. In essence, the company makes a scientific wager on a new customer's potential value—and then treats the customer accordingly. When a customer signs up for the airline's Executive Club, the customer's profile is modeled against the club's 1.5 million members. Based on the results, the airline then predicts which of the club's three tier levels the customer eventually will achieve—blue, silver or gold. "Rather than waiting and watching customers' behavior *before* rewarding them, we treat them differently up front. We *expect* them to behave in a certain way and so we're willing to spend the extra time, money and energy on them. We *incent* the behavior out of them."

For example, it's not uncommon for travelers to receive their frequent flyer club cards five or six weeks after signing up. If British Airways's predictive modeling turns up a potential MVC among its newest recruits, that customer will receive a personalized letter *within days,* thanking him for signing up and welcoming him to the club. The letter will also specifically list advantages and perks offered in the club's higher tiers. The process of one-to-one marketing begins from Day One, instead of waiting until the customer irrevocably proves his or her worth.

"Then we identify those folks who are living up to our expectations. We thank them and reward them with random acts of kindness such as a duty-free voucher or a lounge pass," says Harford. The airline also identifies club members who are buying tickets but aren't delivering relative to the predictive model. These "underachievers" receive a letter offering incentives such as extra miles or special deals for travel companions. The airline saves its most aggressive approach for new club members who model well—and buy nothing. "We really try to get these people off the dime. We'll use the full range of available options to show these folks that we truly want their business. But we make sure that we're spending the right amount of money against the right type of people." So far, the program seems to be working. British Airways has experienced revenue gains among customers identified as possessing higher revenue potential, compared to a control group.

This approach also helps the airline cope with a problem common to frequent flyer loyalty programs—if a customer doesn't activate the program within ninety days of signing up, the chances of growing a relationship with that customer are greatly diminished. It's terribly important to remember that, when a company is selling a perishable—and let's face it, an airline ticket is perishable—one of the most powerful competitive edges is the relative quality of the buyer-seller relationship. In other words, is the company doing all it can to get, keep and grow high-value customers? Traditionalists can shake their heads at the share price of Amazon stock, but the fact remains that customer relationships now have a perceived value on Wall Street. So is it any surprise that some of the world's best airlines are jumping through hoops to earn the loyalty of their Most Valuable Customers?

On a more mundane level, Harford's 1to1 approach to

managing customer relationships has delivered measurable efficiencies that reinforce his team's efforts. "Let's get real. If we grow our program at 15 percent per year, that doesn't mean we can grow our budget 15 percent per year. That just doesn't fly anymore. So we have to figure out how to be more effective and more efficient with the money we've got." Operationally, that translates into anticipating customer expectations—and exceeding them.

Convinced the opportunity for uninterrupted sleeping is something business travelers value above all other creature comforts, British Airways offers business class passengers the chance to dine in the lounge *before* boarding. "It costs us a bit more money, but it helps our customers maximize their travel experience. We're also expanding our arrival lounges in London. We have 45 individual shower stalls, snooze rooms, gymnasium, full breakfast—it's unbelievable! But that's what many of our customers want—to sleep all the way through their flight, take a shower, get a real breakfast and head off to their meetings. The important thing is that British Airways enables travelers to choose the type of experience they want, allowing them as much control over their environment as possible."

In the ongoing battle for air supremacy, British Airways has learned that caring for customers has to become a way of life. Everyone at the firm has to live it, breathe it, walk it and talk it. But making this happen is not always a simple thing, which is why the airline has people like Woody Harford.

Company: Nabisco (PARSIPPANY, NEW JERSEY)

Pioneer: Silvio Bonvini, senior manager of new media, LifeSavers Co.

Lesson: Even if you are legally or ethically restricted in terms of how you collect and use individual customer information, you can still create a smarter marketing program by interacting with your customers more.

Sometimes organizations may face restrictions that prevent them from taking full advantage of the Web. Some managers face situations where conditions beyond their control force them to take a slower, more guarded approach to implementing a customer management plan. That shouldn't necessarily stop an organization from creating a great Web site that incorporates many one-to-one features.

A fine example of this is Nabisco's highly entertaining, lavishly produced LifeSavers Candystand Web site *(www.candystand.com)*, which features a remarkably rich variety of interactive games primarily designed to interest children and teenagers.

Developed by Skyworks Technologies of Maywood, New Jersey, the award-winning site contains more than 27 Shockwave games, as well as informational features and contest promotions. Candystand is divided into 11 themed sections, each dedicated to a particular LifeSavers brand.

Because it's aimed at children and teenagers, however, the site is highly restricted in terms of its ability to collect information. Candystand attracts more than 300,000 unique visitors a month, but it doesn't generate hard customer data. "Our goal is to create an exciting online experience that reflects the fun and quality associated with the LifeSavers brands," explains Silvio Bonvini, senior manager of new media at LifeSavers Co. "For the production cost of about two television spots we have a marketing vehicle that lives twenty-four hours a day, seven days a week, three hundred sixty-five days a year."

The innovative site offers LifeSavers a wonderfully efficient channel for collecting highly valuable customer feedback. Candystand includes a feature called "What Do You Think?" Clicking on it brings up a list of open-ended questions that generated 225,000 responses in just over a year's time. "It's instant communication that we pass along directly to our brand people," says Bonvini. "It's not filtered by an agency or edited in any way. It's verbatim feedback from consumers that we consider incredibly valuable." Based on comments collected from the Web site, LifeSavers brand managers were able to improve packaging in the case of one product and help argue successfully in favor of resurrecting the abandoned wintergreen flavor in the Carefree sugarless gum line.

This kind of interactivity represents a tremendously savvy use of the Internet's inherent power. But is this 1to1 marketing? No, it's not. On the other hand, it's definitely the case that the more you know about your customers, the smarter you'll be in terms of marketing to them. Offering an open-ended online survey allows LifeSavers to do some highly intelligent marketing research based on up-to-the-minute knowledge of its customers. It may not be "one-to-one" marketing, by a strict definition of the term, but it's very smart marketing nonetheless.

The restrictions—both voluntary and legal—hamper the site's ability to deliver a completely one-to-one experience. "We are compliant with the strict guidelines set forth by CARU (Children's Advertising Review Unit), and this handcuffs our ability to capture as much information about consumers as we would like. We don't use cookie technology and all the information we've gathered to date has been voluntary," says Bonvini. "It can be frustrating, because we have the perfect medium for a one-to-one relationship with our customers, yet we are limited in our ability to determine who they are."

Despite these obstacles, the site is an important marketing tool for LifeSavers. The company recently "debuted" its new CremeSaver candy on the Web site, offering a free roll to the first 10,000 people who agreed to participate in a marketing survey. "Everything is being done online—except mailing the candy, of course. We expect an 80 percent response. If we had used traditional marketing tactics, the response probably would be 3 percent to 5 percent," says Bonvini. "And it would have cost a heck of a lot more."

Pretty impressive, especially considering the severe restrictions imposed on the site. And most organizations don't face this kind of limitation. So, looking out over the infinite expanse of cyberspace, the real question that emerges is, why aren't more companies taking full advantage of the Web to interact with *their* customers?

Company: CrossWorlds Software
(BURLINGAME, CALIFORNIA)

Pioneer: Katrina Garnett, CEO

Lesson: Putting a human face on your firm can make a big difference. Even if you have to hire Richard Avedon to prove it.

Sometimes, the hardest word to say to a customer is "no." Katrina Garnett, the founder and CEO of Cross-Worlds Software, knows how to say no—even when her customers want to say yes. It's not contrariness—it's discipline. "The customers and the products have to match. We end up saying no to a lot of customers who aren't in our sweet spot." The law of supply and demand also plays a role. A spate of mergers in the telecom industry has hiked demand for Garnett's product: specialized software that integrates a variety of business processes and applications such as enterprise resource planning, supply chain management and human resources. So the temptation is to run out and sign up new customers—even if there's no product ready at the shipping dock. But this would violate two Garnett principles. First, it would go against the grain of the company's revenue recognition model. The model ensures smoother, more predictable revenue streams—the kind seasoned IT investors now look for. Second, it would be personally embarrassing for Garnett, who makes a point of meeting all the company's customers. "It's pretty much a face-to-face relationship," she says.

Garnett took the face-to-face aspect to a new extreme by paying celebrity photographer Richard Avedon to shoot her in glamour poses that became the centerpiece of a worldwide print media campaign. "Actually, it was my husband's idea. We wanted to put a face on the company. Our products are so complex that it's hard to communicate your message on a single page. This cuts through the noise. It says, 'I own the company, get to know me.' The customers are saying, 'I've got software, what I need is a relationship. I want to know whom I'm dealing with before I make a commitment.'"

The $1 million campaign apparently struck a nerve. Hits on the CrossWorlds Web site jumped from 150,000 per month to 1.5 million. Dozens of articles appeared in newspapers and magazines commenting on the ads. Thousands of calls poured in, many of them from prospective customers.

While Garnett's coup wasn't exactly 1to1, it created the opportunity for—and indeed the expectation of—a personalized relationship. Garnett quickly leveraged the opportunity, mounting a vigorous outbound calling campaign to reach Fortune 500 CIOs while her image was still fresh in their minds. The calls resulted in a 25 percent response rate from the CIOs. Qualified leads were passed along to Garnett, who personally handled the follow-up calls or visits to prospective customers. "The campaign opened the door for us. We have more than 300 very qualified accounts in our pipeline; we can't get to them all."

The mother of three young children, Garnett sees the

campaign and resultant attention as a small jump forward for society. "A lot of women CIOs told me they were glad I didn't compromise my femininity. Many of these women feel like they have to dress the part to conform to the corporate culture they're in. I said, 'I don't feel the need to do that, I'm not a nerd.' It goes back to being a good role model. I took the risk and it turned out to be tremendously successful."

Thought Generator
Knowing the Customer

Can your organization tailor specific messages to specific customers—the way Mercedes-Benz does with its M-Class promotion—or does everyone get the same message? If you were able to send tailored messages, who would get which message? How could you adjust messages based on what you know about each customer? And how might you integrate customer-specific campaign management into the rest of your operation?

For example, if you had particular customers "lined up" for particular messages, would you be able to recognize those customers when they dial your call center (for their own reasons), so you could deliver the message or make the offer at that time?

Is the customer information you acquire really used to improve customer relationships—or is it simply stored somewhere? Following the lead of Dick's Supermarkets, how would your firm go about using the information you have about a specific customer to change the way you actually treat that customer?

In the business-to-business environment, collecting information on individuals is often difficult. Whom might British Airways want to know within your organization? What information about them would be important for British Airways?

Who, if anyone, represents the customer at various decision points in your organization? At British Airways, Woody Harford's job is to serve as "customer advocate." Could your firm implement such a position? You have a Chief Executive Officer and a Chief Financial Officer—should you (could you) have a Chief Customer Officer?

Could Dick's Supermarkets jump-start a Learning Relationship with its customers? How? Could they adopt the "projecting" techniques pioneered by British Airways, in order to start treating first-time or second-time customers at a level appropriate for their eventual, expected spending pattern?

Customer loyalty can be generated by enhancing the experience of purchasing, using or interacting with your product. If, as is the case with Nabisco's LifeSavers division, there are regulatory or other issues that prevent you from engaging in actual, one-to-one relationships with your customers, then enhancing the product experience may be all that's available. What could you do to make the experience of interacting with your company, product or service more interesting, more interactive, or just more fun?

Katrina Garnett launched a global ad campaign to remind customers and prospects they would be dealing with human beings at her software company. Does *your* organization need a human face?

Please e-mail responses to
knowing@1to1.com

Respecting the Channel

I t's one thing to deal with the organization of your own firm, or its culture or the general level of knowledge with respect to CRM principles. This is hard enough, but it's manageable.

On the other hand, many companies sell through channel partners—and when there are dealers, distributors, resellers, retailers, or other channel members between you and your end-user customer, then launching a one-to-one marketing initiative can be much more difficult.

It is possible that the channel you sell through has already outlived its usefulness and is being replaced or pushed aside by new technologies and other business models—such as, for instance, an e-commerce site or direct-to-consumer call center, relying on FedEx for its logistics. If new-entrant competitors in your business category are going direct to end-users while you are using a more traditional distribution channel structure, then be careful. All may not be lost, but all is certainly at risk. Yes, going direct yourself almost certainly will involve cannibalizing some of your own business, but whom would you rather be eaten by?

On the other hand, if you have channel partners who serve a clear purpose, over and above the mere inventorying and delivery of products to end-users, then you should probably be using the principles of one-to-one marketing to strengthen and deepen your relationships with these partners. You should be helping your partners to create better relationships with their own customers (who are your end-user customers), to your mutual benefit. You should provide tools and resources to enable your channel partners to deliver your product or service better, more intelligently, less expensively, more efficiently.

Both strategies are valid, whether you choose to go around the channel or strengthen your relationships within it. It's only a question of what fits your particular business situation.

Company: Xerox (STAMFORD, CONNECTICUT)

Pioneer: *Nina Smith, vice-president of integrated corporate marketing*

Lesson: *Setting up relationships with customers across multiple channels can be very difficult. There's no easy solution, but one thing is certain: Your customers want it to happen, so it will happen. The only real question is whether or not you will be doing it.*

Until recently, the only time most people used the word "channel" around the hallways and corridors at Xerox was when they were talking about last night's TV programs. Nowadays you're more likely to hear the word used in its marketing sense.

One of Xerox's larger corporate clients is American Express. High-end Xerox printers and copiers crowd out the competition at AmEx's data processing centers. It's a lucrative account. A sales rep, a global account rep and a top-level Xerox executive all keep their eyes on the account to make sure Amex stays happy. But when American Express needed mid-range or low-range printers, it wasn't buying them from Xerox.

"We were missing a whole chunk of their business," explains Nina Smith, Xerox's vice-president of integrated corporate marketing. "If you were an office manager at Amex, you were buying printers and copiers through distributors and dealers. But Xerox didn't work with distributors and dealers, so guess what? We missed that piece of the market because customers did not like to buy those products through a direct sales force. Let's face it, if you have a sales rep come in and talk to you about the features and functionality of some product, there's more overhead involved and you're going to wind up paying for it. So I don't want to tell you the only way you can buy from us is if you sit down with a direct sales rep. Because chances are, if you're looking for a $2,000 printer, you're going to walk into a store or go out on the Internet—and just buy it."

Wresting this huge opportunity away from established competitors meant Xerox would have to determine not only what kind of products its customers wanted but also *how* they wanted to buy them. When it became clear that some customers simply would not purchase the complete range of Xerox products through a direct sales force, Xerox realized it was time to cultivate a variety of *indirect* sales channels such as dealerships, distributors, value-added resellers, telemarketing and e-commerce. "The customers are the decision makers. Our job is to help them buy the way they *want* to buy," says Smith, who readily concedes that the transition from a purely direct sales model to a model that mixes direct sales and channel sales has been difficult. "The direct sales force felt extremely threatened by the introduction of new channels."

The company's initial approach to allaying those fears didn't help. If someone at American Express wanted to buy one of Xerox's new 32-page-per-minute printers, which sells for about $3,000, the Xerox direct sales rep would be asked to handle the sale and turn the order over to a distributor for fulfillment, in return for a small "finder's fee." But since such finder's fees didn't count against the revenue quotas each sales rep was striving to meet, they weren't very enthusiastic about the program.

According to Smith, "Initially we said we wouldn't comp the sales reps for selling the printer, we'd give them a finder's fee instead, say $100 for each printer sold. But now we incent them to partner with the distributors and the dealers directly. And we give them actual revenue credit for the transaction. It counts on their revenue plan. We're going to continue on this course, because you really can't underestimate the value of the direct channel as a vehicle for creating demand. The direct channel already has a relationship with the customer. What they don't have is *all* the relationships they need to maximize that account."

Smith is confident that Xerox can make good on the promise it made back in 1992 to become more than just a big company that makes copiers. In that year the staid corporation embarked on a quest to reinvent itself as "The Document Company." A snazzy new logo was introduced to suggest an image of Xerox as a vital player in the Information Age. There were internal shake-ups, reorganizations and restructurings. Rick Thoman was tapped to succeed Paul Allaire as CEO.

Back in the corporate trenches, however, it was managers such as Smith who were charged with the arduous labor of nudging the company onto its new course. The oldest of six children in a single-parent home, Smith learned early in life to be creative. "I think back to my childhood. We didn't have a lot of money. If I had a school project and I couldn't afford to buy all the pieces I needed to put it together, I'd go into the kitchen with my mom and we'd figure out how to do it with what we had." Smith sees plenty of similarities between assembling a school science project and devising a workable marketing strategy. "You have to be creative, you have to imagine all the pieces and see how they fit together in the big picture. Then you've got to get people to pay attention, understand it *and* want to become a part of it."

One of Smith's assignments is to develop a methodology for managing customer relationships with chief information officers. "Think about this: Xerox now makes products that sit on the network, affecting the customer's entire information technology infrastructure. So you're not just talking about sitting down with the purchasing agent anymore. You really have to change the way you go to market. You need new contact points inside the account and you need new relationships. That's why we're working on a strategy for marketing to CIOs. Why should a CIO care about Xerox? Well, if you've got corporate e-mail, chances are you've got network printers, and if those printers go down, who's going to get called? The CIO."

Xerox also has begun to develop integrated account strategies, enabling its managers to address several aspects of a customer's universe of needs simultaneously. In this scenario, an account manager would supervise an integrated team made up of representatives from direct sales, indirect channels, document services, product teams and other key areas, depending on the customer's needs. Essentially, an enterprise-wide team would be charged with proposing solutions to meet the customer's enterprise-wide needs. Xerox has also created a corporate-level integrated marketing organization whose role is to harmonize products and services that cross functional boundaries.

Led by Smith, this new organization is responsible for ensuring that a consistent message is delivered across all segments of the company's global market. It's a heavy burden, she concedes. "But the important thing is that we are recognizing the need for integration."

Allaire agrees, arguing that this approach has "strengthened the Xerox brand without compromising divisional product strategies." Allaire says the process of change has already become self-organizing, thanks in part to improved company-wide communications that make it easier for managers to share best practices. What remains to be seen, however, is just how far Xerox is willing to push the envelope. Will the entire enterprise evolve toward becoming one fully integrated entity, with a consistent approach to managing customer relationships? Or will the effort stop when it threatens established turf?

Come what may, Smith is delighted to serve as pilot. "We're charting a new course. At Xerox, the focus has been on sales and we've done extremely well with that focus. There hasn't really been a focus on marketing, so everything I do is something that hasn't been done before. It's a really great feeling. It's also a little scary, because you never know when you might get into something that doesn't work. It's a learning experience."

Her advice to other managers with similar new responsibilities is simple and direct: Never lose your credibility within the organization. "I believe the reason I have been successful is that I can go to any business group president, or I can go to any of our field operations presidents, and I can sit down and explain the rationale for a new program. I can explain to them why they should relinquish control of a particular program, why it's better for the company. You have to be a facilitator, someone who can bring people to the table."

But once you've got them there, she warns, you must deliver the goods. "You're going to be stepping on a lot of toes. I tell my team that we will have no meeting with anyone unless we have something valuable to deliver. And we've held to that—we deliver."

Company: Hewlett-Packard
(PALO ALTO, CALIFORNIA)

Pioneer: Shirley Choy-Marshall, marketing program manager

Lesson: Setting up a consumer-oriented Web site has the potential for seriously disrupting existing sales channels. But even if the channel issues are dealt with skillfully, a product-centric firm trying to set up a customer-centric Web site must hammer out its interdivisional conflicts.

While Shirley Choy-Marshall was still a teenager in San Jose, she decided she would become an architect. "I was enamored with the challenge of taking intangibles and turning them into something real," she says. She followed her dream, studied architecture and joined a small design firm. A few years later, when the practical challenges of architecture had grown less appealing, she returned to school, earned an MBA and discovered the rapidly expanding world of e-commerce.

"It was 1996 and the Internet was just beginning to

take off. I was fortunate to jump in at the right time. It was all so new and exciting. We felt like we were creating the rules, trying all kinds of new things and making history."

In 1998, she joined Hewlett-Packard's Consumer Products Business Organization in Santa Clara. Her formal training in architecture—with its emphasis on transforming ideas into forms—serves her well at HP, where she works with a team of creative thinkers whose assignment is designing and building the company's consumer Web site, HP Shopping Village *(www.shopping.hp.com)*.

On the surface, HP Shopping Village resembles many other transactional Web sites aimed at consumers. It features a library of customer-friendly information and an array of products available for purchase online, including printers, PCs, toner cartridges, digital cameras, scanners and so forth. Visitors can sign up for a free e-mail newsletter about new store offerings. What's noteworthy about HP Shopping Village is not what visitors to the site see—it's what they *don't* see. HP Shopping Village is, without exaggeration, the small tip of a very large iceberg.

To a greater extent than most other corporations its size, Hewlett-Packard has decentralized its many divisions and product lines. Over several decades, this global decentralization has proved a source of immense strength and resiliency. It allows Hewlett-Packard to move rapidly and compete effectively in a marketplace that mutates at warp speed.

But this structure has its drawbacks, too. On the one hand it gives HP's managers the freedom to experiment and innovate. But on the other hand such decentralization makes it difficult for these managers to collaborate on customer-specific activities, because they function independently, in separate, product-oriented silos. Despite efforts by top management to integrate key functions such as sales and marketing, the fact remains that HP's divisional managers have difficulty communicating across the gaps dividing them.

However, in the new global marketplace, where strong customer relationships are emerging as a critical measure of success, Hewlett-Packard's decentralization makes it very difficult for the firm to present a consistent appearance to an individual customer. In 1997, the company launched a special initiative to pull its consumer product lines closer together. The initiative resulted in a more unified approach to advertising, packaging and messaging. HP's consumer e-commerce effort is one important step in this direction, says Shen Li, general manager of HP Shopping Village.

Although HP Shopping Village was not created for this express purpose, it does serve as a crucible for resolving interdivisional conflicts, a virtual laboratory for implementing an integrated marketing strategy. "We are a bridge that crosses the gaps between the product organizations," says Li. "As a result, we constantly face an enormous challenge—providing a consistent, unified experience for a wide variety of customers with a wide variety of individual needs. We've found the Internet to be a wonderful tool to harness the power of the various product lines and translate that power into a cohesive customer experience."

Indeed, HP Shopping Village embodies two striking

advantages. First, it clearly represents an answer to the unmet needs of many HP customers and prospects who prefer to shop online. "Our extensive research shows that 20 percent of U.S. consumers purchase PCs direct from the manufacturer," says Li. A significant portion of these consumers prefer buying *exclusively* from the manufacturer, citing brand reputation and flexibility of the Web as a shopping medium.

Second, HP Shopping Village is one of the few places where consumers can view Hewlett-Packard's full range of desktop and home office products. So if you want to buy an HP Pavilion PC, an HP DeskJet printer, an HP PhotoSmart digital camera, an HP hand calculator *and* an extra supply of toner, you can do it all at HP Shopping Village.

"Our goal is to be the market leader in the consumer PC and peripheral business. Therefore, we need to offer our products where customers want to buy them," says Li.

Sounds simple, right? Find out where your customers are and be there for them when they want to buy.

The only problem is that if your company already has one or two or many sales channels, the Web is likely to represent a threat—or at best a challenge—to those channels. At HP, the real task is figuring out how to make the Web channel work without alienating a worldwide army of commissioned salespeople, retailers, wholesalers, value-added resellers, strategic partners and systems integrators.

Despite these hurdles, HP Shopping Village is moving ahead—carefully and in stages. The current site actually had a short-lived predecessor: HP Outlet Center. That

site, which sold refurbished products and printing supplies, served as a training ground for HP's current direct
sales effort.

When it came time to assemble the current site, Li
and his team took an incremental approach, starting
small and learning along the way. One success led to
another. The major consumer product lines led the way,
which is not surprising when you consider the competition they face from Dell, Gateway and Compaq. These
product divisions jumped at the chance to sell direct and
were very aggressive. When other consumer divisions saw
products selling well through HP Shopping Village, they
felt more comfortable with the idea and signed on. Grad-
ually, HP Shopping Village expanded its lineup of offerings, which now includes products for the office.

"Now there's a vast level of participation from numer-
ous product lines," says Li. "This level of buy-in allows us
to bundle HP products and offer special packages, which
is a good thing for us and our customers."

HP's retail partners have taken the online develop-
ments in stride. "They realize this is the wave of the
future and they expect us to sell online. HP will continue
to provide a choice of channels for customers, which is
why we continue to support and invest in building the
online selling initiatives of our partners. Additionally, if
you can't find what you want at HP Shopping Village,
you'll find a link to a page that will help you locate a
reseller. Even though we believe that direct selling will
someday become something very big, we respect the existing channels. Our mission is better coverage—both
offline and online," says Li.

Although HP won't talk on the record about pricing strategy, it's no secret that the online store tries hard not to undersell its brick and mortar counterparts. Clearly, the strategy is to be on par with the average, not the lowest and not the highest, just somewhere in between.

While this pricing strategy offers comfort to HP's other sales channels, it runs the risk of offending shoppers who visit HP Shopping Village expecting steep discounts from the manufacturer.

Evidently, that's a risk HP is willing to take. Discounts attract precisely the kind of customers 1to1 managers *don't* want. If it's set up correctly, a 1to1 Web site will attract customers for a host of reasons other than low prices.

Online direct selling offers the opportunity to form relationships that last beyond the initial transaction. "I've noticed that people feel that if they buy direct, they have a sense of relationship and that because of that relationship, many of the intangibles surrounding the product will be better," says Choy-Marshall.

The HP Shopping Village team is taking steps to ensure that visitors leave the site with that sense of relationship intact. "We just launched an area on the site called 'My Printing Supplies Store.' It's aimed at people who find it confusing to shop for printing supplies—which is pretty much everybody. You can tell us about your printing needs by specifying up to two HP printers that you own and every time you come back to the site, we'll show you the supplies that apply to your needs. We'll also show you project ideas and tips to make your own particular printing chores easier."

Choy-Marshall says that 'My Printing Supplies Store' is a prototype for the future. She and her team hope to extend relationship-building features to other areas of HP Shopping Village. Eventually, she says, the entire site will feature one-to-one capabilities. Hewlett-Packard chose BroadVision, the same firm that developed the American Airlines site, to develop HP Shopping Village, because of the company's proven experience with online relationship management issues.

"Relationship building is the differentiating factor that will make people trust us, come back to us and tell their friends about us. By now, we all know that it's much more cost efficient to service a repeat customer than to acquire a new one. Relationships will be our strongest asset—and they will be exceedingly difficult for our competitors to replicate," says Choy-Marshall.

Company: Great Plains
(FARGO, NORTH DAKOTA)

Pioneer: *Tracy Faleide, general manager of services and sales*
Lesson: *When selling through indirect channels, it pays to use one-to-one marketing principles with your channel partners, involving them in more and more collaborative relationships with your firm. Your goal should be to enable your channel partners to treat* their *customers in a one-to-one fashion, and then motivate them to do so.*

Tracy Faleide knows what it means to have a one-to-one relationship with a company. Take, for example, the time

she ordered a holiday flower arrangement for her grandparents who live in Canby, Faleide's small hometown in
southwestern Minnesota.

"So I called this business. They know me. They know
my mom and dad. And I said, 'I need to send flowers to
my grandparents, Richard and Donna, at the nursing
home. And send another arrangement to my other
grandmother, Irene.'"

Faleide was about to give the florist the addresses. "She
said, 'That's okay, we know where they are.'"

As Faleide goes about her job as general manager of
services and sales for Great Plains of Fargo, North Da-
kota, she brings those small-town lessons with her. She
wants to make sure that every one of Great Plains's customers, prospective customers, employees, and channel
partners feels as though they have an intimate, one-to-
one relationship with the company.

Great Plains sells mid-range accounting and management solution packages. If your 300-person law firm or
manufacturing plant wants to install a new payroll system
to run on a Microsoft SQL Server, chances are good that
it will be a Great Plains package. These products, while
virtually "shrink wrapped," when compared to more complicated corporate system upgrades and installations,
nevertheless require some amount of consulting and integration work, both on the front end and on the back.
Usually a reseller partner—a firm that might consult on
accounting and financial control issues, for instance—will
work with the customer to install and implement the solution, streamlining business processes along the way.
They provide customized training and other services to

ensure a successful implementation. And they typically provide ongoing technical support during and after the implementation, working collaboratively with Great Plains to meet the customer's needs. "Because our products are highly customizable, and because customers often revamp and streamline their business processes during implementation, all of our sales go through about 1,500 reseller partners," explains Faleide.

In one sense, these reseller partners are themselves Great Plains's real customers. They're the ones Great Plains deals with on a daily basis, the ones that "take delivery" of the company's product. But in another, equally valid sense, the companies that buy the installations from the reseller partners are the customers, because they're the ones driving real demand for the product. And within any corporate customer there are several individuals with various levels of influence or control over the purchase decision. As is true of any business-to-business marketer, Great Plains could easily think of these individuals as customers too.

The fact is, Great Plains must work to cement its relationships with each of these sets of customers, and this can get complicated very quickly. For instance, in most cases, a request for information or a complaint will go first to the installing reseller, but sometimes it might come directly to Great Plains. So how should the company get such an inquiry to the appropriate reseller, on a timely basis? And is there any way to make sure a reseller has all the information needed?

For Great Plains, the answer was creating an interactive communication to bind its reseller partners ever closer to the firm. The service must be designed to ensure that a reseller speaks with the same "voice" as Great Plains, so that the corporate or end-user customer gets a unified, coherent, rational view of any transaction. Only in this way can Great Plains go on to the task of ensuring long-term dialogue continuity, which is necessary for building Learning Relationships and cementing the customer's loyalty. An interaction with a customer today must pick up where the dialogue with that particular customer left off yesterday.

VOICE, an acronym for Virtual Organization Information Center, represents Great Plains's principal effort in dealing with these issues. An ambitious, Web-based information system, VOICE offers detailed information profiles on key contacts within partner organizations and their assigned customers, product information, installation and usage tips, training course material and even job placement ads. Names. Phone numbers. Sales figures by time periods and product line. Customer satisfaction ratings. Resellers using VOICE can see nearly everything Great Plains has in its own records, including serial numbers, registration keys, call history, service log and the customer's record of past interactions with both Great Plains and the reseller. So, whether the customer calls Great Plains or the company they bought the solution from, everyone is working with the same information.

Another important element of Great Plains's program is the manner in which the company has approached the marketing decision-making process. While many companies look at customers solely in terms of the products they buy, Great Plains has found it more effective to slice marketing information along the customer dimension. So customers are grouped by industry, by growth rate, by revenue to Great Plains, by the needs expressed to Great Plains, by the number of service calls made and even by the type of corporate culture.

This allows the firm to zero in on customers and treat them differently based on what they need and what they're worth to Great Plains. Just as important as being able to recognize those "ideal" customers—customers who are loyal, profitable and collaborative—is being able to identify nonprofitable and at-risk customers, so they can be treated appropriately. Once customers are grouped into the right categories, Great Plains can then cross-tabulate against customer satisfaction and loyalty data, in order to make sure its picture is complete.

An important part of this "customer knowledge" development process is the customer survey and feedback program at Great Plains. Internet-based surveys ask customers if they need additional information, services or attention. The survey also asks open-ended questions, such as, "What is the most important thing Great Plains can do to improve your business success?" Overall, these surveys allow the company to develop customized solutions for customers when concerns or problems crop up.

While putting to use all the information it collects about its customers, the company has found that it is not enough just to disseminate the data, or even summaries of the data. Instead, it quickly became apparent that a cost-efficient process for prioritizing the information was needed, so that the company and its channel partners could respond appropriately to each issue, with the least amount of wasted effort, and the most effort expended on the most important issues.

"One of the things we found was that our system required our partners to go out and look for the right information," says Faleide. "That could be very time-consuming. We wanted an easy way to be notified if a customer had called into the support team and needed some extra attention."

Rather than having to wade through tons of raw data each day to see who called and why, Great Plains decided to prioritize the information by urgency and customer type. When a call comes in from a customer, the company's support technicians log the call history. When that information is entered into the database, it is also e-mailed, automatically, to the appropriate customer account manager at whatever partner organization has responsibility for that customer.

However, if a customer has called and is upset about something, or the technicians determine that the customer needs some extra support and attention for any reason, the e-mail is flagged as "urgent." The e-mail is also marked "urgent" if the technician's judgment is that the interaction represents a business opportunity.

"So," Faleide says, "whether it's a problem or a new-business opportunity, what comes across is a high-priority visual clue. It is the type of customer interaction we and our partners want to know about and respond to right away. We don't want it getting lost in a pile of routine e-mails."

Putting this program into place required the firm to rethink the way it monitored progress and measured success. The company has had to acknowledge and deal with the reality that it simply takes more time for a technician to render this kind of analysis and support. Since the company also tracks incoming call rates, response times and other "cost-based" statistics to measure the success of customer support at the technical end, Faleide says there has been an "adjustment period."

"We are working hard to communicate the benefits of this system and share success stories," Faleide says. "We get partners and customers thanking us all the time, and we circulate these notes. We're able to deliver specialized attention to individual customers, and to customize our responses, all because of this system."

And finally, in addition to the technical systems, the business processes, and the success measurements considered, Great Plains also had to educate its people. The company is now teaching *all* its employees about the principles of CRM and 1to1 marketing. The firm is asking employees to embrace the basic idea and to devise new ways to put these principles to work.

"This education has been across the company, not just in the marketing department," says Faleide. "We want everyone to understand one-to-one concepts and how they can apply them to their everyday jobs. It's going to change the way we do business. It's going to change their individual roles and their teams' roles. Everything will change as we continue to implement this new way of doing business."

The training program itself provides an object lesson in the benefits of 1to1 marketing. For instance, Pam McGee, a member of the corporate education team and co-trainer of 1to1 business practices along with Faleide, sends personalized messages to employees about training classes. These messages will take into account any training that employee has had before, and will emphasize the benefits of additional training. The firm has found this to be much more effective at promoting course attendance, when compared to the "old" method of issuing generic, one-size-fits-all invitations. McGee also sends personalized notes to employees who attend the classes, thanking them for their participation and following up on their ideas and questions. These personal touches help the company maintain a high level of enthusiasm among employees. It also offers a vivid demonstration of the power of personalized communications.

So, on the surface it might seem that Great Plains has a simpler, more easily understood business model, with a limited number of "customers" that take delivery of its product and resell it to their customers. But scratch the surface of this business model and you see that the management of customer relationships at this firm is no less complex than it would be at nearly any other. It involves the same need to blend technology with business processes and training, and it poses the same challenges to the way the firm communicates internally and measures its own success.

But it is no less important to the long-term success of Great Plains. In the software industry, Faleide says, it's easy to be replaced if you offer nothing more than a product.

"As software products continue to be more commoditized," she says, "our value will come more from the relationships we have with our customers. And customers are starting to get used to higher levels of personalized service in all areas of their lives. Not only do they expect it, they demand it."

Thought Generator
Respecting the Channel

Progress, it seems, creates as many problems as it solves. As the economy evolves to embrace the online universe, many companies suddenly find themselves facing channel conflicts. Helping to resolve these conflicts will be a key duty for any one-to-one manager.

Managing a Learning Relationship across a multi-tiered distribution channel requires teamwork. Can you think of activities or programs that might engender this type of cooperation? What steps could your organization take to reduce the anxiety salespeople are likely to feel when they are required to work more closely with channel members?

Let's consider the example of Great Plains, which cultivates mutually beneficial, one-to-one relationships with its channel partners. Would your channel members describe their relationships with your organization in the same way? If not, what steps could you take to begin converting your channel members into true partners?

How much of what you know about your customers comes from interacting with your channel members? If the answer is "little or none," what could you do to remedy that situation without triggering fear among channel members?

How would you encourage distributors or dealers to share individual customer information with you? As a manufacturer, are there some channel members who are more important to your success than others? How could you use this fact to make your channel-management program more effective?

One key to Hewlett-Packard's strategy for going direct to consumers with HP Shopping Village is its "middle-of-the-road" pricing policy. Do you agree with this policy? What might be some reasonable alternatives?

Please e-mail responses to
respect@1to1.com

Tool Makers

I t's one thing to sell a product or service to a company that helps it operate better, faster, more cost-efficiently, more safely, or more cleanly. But it's another thing altogether to sell a company something that is used most effectively only when the company changes the way it actually does business.

This is exactly the situation faced by a number of companies now trying to sell their clients software applications, computer hardware, Web services and other useful tools for creating and managing one-to-one customer relationships. The first step in the selling process is to educate the client as to why it would be a good idea to concentrate on CRM issues at all.

Company: DoubleClick
(NEW YORK, NEW YORK)

Pioneer: *Kevin O'Connor, CEO*
Lesson: *To invent new uses for technology, harness the collective intelligence of your workforce. When the product you make allows other companies to harness the Internet's power to treat different customers differently, you'll not only be transforming your company, you'll be transforming the world.*

In Manhattan's Hell's Kitchen, on the West Side, not far from the mouth of the Lincoln Tunnel, there are new offices in a space once occupied by an ice skating rink and methadone clinic. In these offices you'll find the headquarters of a revolutionary, radical movement threatening to alter permanently the face of advertising.

Up on the sixteenth floor of the old Westyard Building, surrounded by a wraparound outdoor terrace, are the new offices of DoubleClick, where a youngish-looking man with round spectacles and the slightly owlish demeanor of a Cambridge don presides over a rebellion against mass marketing.

Kevin O'Connor doesn't look like a revolutionary. An unruly lock of blondish hair falling across his forehead suggests Dennis the Menace more than Che Guevera. In his youth, O'Connor collected old radios and TV sets, scavenging the components to "build weird stuff," such as a light-powered telephone and an electronic raccoon repellant. His boyhood hero was Thomas Edison, a man driven to experiments and inventions.

Cofounder and CEO of DoubleClick, O'Connor has set his sights on remaking the $400-billion-a-year market for worldwide advertising—one customer at a time.

DoubleClick itself represents an effort to bring manageability to the fast-growing—some would say chaotic—field of Internet-based advertising. The company's online reporting techniques allow advertisers to measure how well or how poorly their campaigns are performing and what types of users are seeing and clicking on their ads. The company enables its clients to use their ads to appeal to individual consumers, one at a time, instead of trying to target market segments.

"Imagine if all the ads in *Time* magazine changed just for you," says O'Connor. "And imagine if *Time* could know that you saw the ad, how you responded to it, whether you actually purchased any products and how many products you purchased. That would be pretty amazing."

O'Connor and his team are moving toward achieving this vision in cyberspace. DoubleClick's premier product is called DART, which stands for Dynamic Advertising Reporting and Targeting. "When a user goes to a Web page, we determine at that moment what ad they're going to see based on their environment and what we know about them," says O'Connor. "We manage 7,400 Web sites. We have about 30,000 ad campaigns reaching 48 million users and we deliver billions of ads per month. The system decides who's going to see which ad—so we're taking out the randomness."

"Five years from now, I see DoubleClick being the

clearinghouse for the majority of ads throughout the world, the Sabre reservations system of advertising. You will literally have millions of publishers, tens of millions of advertisers, hundreds of millions of end-users. The only way to manage all that is through some big, world-wide system. If we can pull this off, it will solve an age-old problem of advertising: the problem of determining precisely who's seeing your ad and how they're reacting."

O'Connor's internal management techniques are consistent with the company's external mission. Product development at DoubleClick is an exercise in controlled fusion—somewhat unpredictable but highly energetic. Employees call it the "Kevin Method." The first part of the process is a directed form of brainstorming in which managers are called together from various parts of the company to share ideas and experiences. No idea is considered too extreme for discussion.

O'Connor recently convened one of these brainstorming sessions to shape a new database product for media planners. "All the answers are in this room—we've just got to squeeze them out of you," he happily tells a group of eleven managers. Grabbing a marker, O'Connor plants himself next to a large erasable whiteboard and asks everyone to start talking—about the new product. Within minutes, he's written down a list of 33 essential attributes for the database. The managers then vote for the top 11, which O'Connor dutifully records. "You know what's great about this process?" he tells the managers. "You don't even remember which idea is yours and which is someone else's. When you walk out of this room you'll think you invented this product!"

Now that the product attributes have been roughly defined, O'Connor guides the managers through the next five stages of the development process—placement (sales), promotion (marketing), positioning, pricing and partners. Each stage begins with a period of unedited brainstorming, followed by a vote winnowing the ideas to just a few. After two and a half hours the managers have fleshed out a new product. The result of their labor is then subjected to an exhaustive round of market analysis to determine its actual viability.

"Even if we decide not to go ahead with a particular product, the sessions are extremely useful. My basic assumption is that our collective intelligence is more valuable than the sum of everyone's individual intelligence. So almost all of our strategic issues are discussed in this kind of a forum," says O'Connor.

An engineer by training and temperament, O'Connor is undaunted by new technology. "People look at the Internet as very chaotic, when in fact it is not. Moving electrons from one place to another, controlling bits of data—it's actually very easy."

He's comfortable dealing with issues on a granular level. After all, electrons are about as granular as it gets. He's equally comfortable discussing issues on a macro level. "When it comes to technology, I'm an eternal optimist. I think the Internet will bring the end of nationalism and totalitarianism in much the same way that CNN helped bring down the Soviet Union. The Internet enables people to exchange ideas freely. It encourages com-

munication simply by making it easy. You can contact
people all over the world on a daily basis to share information. Just people. No borders."

And no mass advertising.

Company: Oracle
(REDWOOD SHORES, CALIFORNIA)

Pioneer: Neil Mendelson, senior director of data warehousing
Lesson: Selling a company the technology it needs to launch a
   CRM initiative can mean redefining for the company the
   very nature of its own business. Not only does this compli-
   cate the sales process, but it also calls for the selling company to re-think its nature, too.

When Neil Armstrong stepped onto the moon in
1969, Neil Mendelson watched the historic moment on a
large, primitive television set his parents had purchased in
1953. They shipped him the old set recently, along with
the original handwritten receipt for $700. "If you com-
pare that to the $10,000 they paid for their house, you
realize the TV set was a very major purchase," says Mendelson.

Back then, technology was considered exotic, almost
magical. Like a carnival sideshow, it inspired awe, fear
and wonderment. Caught up in this state of wide-
eyed astonishment, millions of families plunked down a
month's pay for their first television set. After all, TV was
a symbol of progress.

Today, as senior director of data warehousing at Oracle, Mendelson sits right on the sharp edge of progress. From his perch he sees the transforming effect of technology on business and, by extension, on society.

One-to-one marketing offers a return to the old days, says Mendelson. "There's something that feels very right about it. People talk about comfort food, which reminds them of their childhood. This kind of marketing is the comfort food of business. It brings us back to the time when we all knew the name of the pharmacist at the corner drugstore."

This popular yearning for "comfort" has a direct effect on Oracle, which supplies critical business software for thousands of companies now racing to develop trusting, personalized relationships with their customers.

"For years, we helped our customers become more efficient. Now our customers are struggling to go beyond efficiency and become more effective," Mendelson explains. "So we need to move with the times as well. It's really a natural evolution. In the beginning we primarily provided database software. Then we offered packaged applications for general ledger, accounts payable, manufacturing and human resources. Then we began offering services to support the enabling technology we provided. You might say we've moved up the value chain with customer relationship management."

The rapidly dropping price of technology has added a sense of urgency to the argument for change. "Like our customers, we confront the challenge of margin erosion. If you go back ten or twelve years, the average cost of software was much higher than it is today. The same holds true for hardware."

Faced with this pressure, it seemed logical for Oracle to expand the definition of its business. This would allow the company to sell a wide range of new products and services to its customers—products and services they would need to compete in the customer dimension, the way new technology allowed them to. And from Oracle's standpoint, the beauty of it was that the CRM trend crosses nearly every industry line, offering the company a broad opportunity to break new ground, in a wide variety of industries.

Banking is just one of several especially promising areas, says Mendelson. "Historically, most banks organized their information technology along product lines. They built separate systems for each of their individual products. As new products came along, they built additional systems to handle them. Today many of those banks are telling us they need a cross-functional customer view, not just a product view."

Mendelson's area of expertise, data warehousing, is focused on enabling organizations to consolidate information from many disparate systems into a single, unified view. This approach makes it possible for a company to analyze a single customer's relationship with the whole enterprise—across a wide range of products and interactions. "We used to talk to our customers about *processing* information for the sake of efficiency. But now we talk to them about *analyzing* information to generate a competitive edge."

Data warehousing creates a unified information view, suggesting a model for a unified customer approach. With access to this kind of information on customers, the people responsible for corporate strategy, marketing, sales, customer service, production and information technology should be able to work together in a more or less seamless, internal partnership. And when they do, it is no longer so easy to define the boundary between marketing and IT, or between sales and customer service.

"The lines are blurring," Mendelson says. "A really good example of where this is happening, functionally, is the call center. A lot of businesses looked at the call center as a *cost* center. But now that people are beginning to focus on their relationships with their customers, and as they realize that these relationships represent the *only* truly sustainable competitive advantage for them, the call center is seen increasingly as an *opportunity* center."

Implication: When you take a customer-oriented view of your situation, not only will you have to redefine your business objective, you might also have to redefine your business. This, of course, immensely complicates the sales process at technology tool makers like Oracle.

But Oracle isn't overly worried about it. The logic of CRM is too irresistible, too inevitable. When an Oracle customer—or any organization, for that matter—wants to embrace one-to-one marketing fully, it must wrestle with its very nature. This necessary struggle creates opportunities for Oracle to raise the level of its relationship with that customer. The onus is on Oracle to stay in synch.

So, with the waves of change swirling around it, Oracle finds itself changing too. "As we begin to really wrestle with the challenges involved in enabling *our* customers to focus on *their* customers, we're presented with a series of new challenges. We need to broaden ourselves immensely. We've always been a company that talks to technology people about technology. But more and more, lately, we find we have to speak to business people about business," says Mendelson.

Like the Apollo space program, which moved closer to its objective by taking a series of small, carefully planned steps, Oracle will almost certainly reach its goal too. It is transforming itself gradually, incrementally, from a technology vendor into a broader, business-issues company. "We're talking about scaling an idea, providing it with the mechanism and the infrastructure to turn it into a reality. That's what we're embarking upon."

Mendelson is justifiably confident. Like the other Neil, he has the resources of a large organization behind him. And like the man he watched on the flickering TV set so many years ago, he knows the best way to move forward is one step at a time. "We're looking at it as a process. It's something we achieve over time."

Company: Sabre Travel Information Network
(FORT WORTH, TEXAS)

Pioneer: *James B. Poage, senior vice-president of worldwide marketing*

Lesson: *Frequent flyer programs are good for building loyalty, but can fall short when it comes to assembling a complete picture of customer activity.*

Jim Poage will never forget his first airplane ride. He was a young boy and an oil company doing business with his dad had sent a plane to ferry the Poage family from Wyoming to Texas. The plane was a DC-3, the graceful twin-propeller craft that defined an earlier, simpler era of air travel. What Poage remembers most about the flight is that he got to sit in the cockpit with the pilots, who smiled warmly, let him touch the controls and even knew his name.

The DC-3 has been obsolete for years, but Poage still clings to the memories of that happy flight. In fact, he's trying hard to make that kind of highly personalized experience a reality for today's air travelers. Poage is the executive champion for one-to-one marketing initiatives at Sabre, which handles almost 40 percent of all the world's airline reservations. "We handle *everything* the traveler does," says Poage.

That gives Sabre a leg up on the airlines, which only know what their own customers are doing. Consequently the airlines don't possess the capability to make real-time decisions based on customer value—something Sabre, with 11,000 employees focused on managing customer information, *can* do.

For example, Northwest Airlines might know that a frequent business traveler routinely takes a 7 A.M. flight whenever she calls on clients in Singapore. But Northwest would have no way of knowing that this same traveler takes her husband and three children to visit relatives in South America every summer. Or that when she flies to Madrid for an annual trade show, she always books a first-class seat on another airline. Sabre, on the other hand, would have a complete picture of this passenger's travel history, as well as her car rental and hotel preferences.

When the traveler calls her travel agent, the agent accesses her profile from Sabre. The agent then passes an electronic version of the profile to the airline, which, at its own discretion, can devise a customized offer likely to win a larger share of the traveler's business. "Let's say the traveler is a titanium card holder on some other airline. Obviously, that's a frequent flyer you want to woo. So you might offer her a complimentary upgrade, special ground services or some other service designed to sway her loyalty."

This virtual omniscience uniquely positions Sabre as a facilitator of one-to-one relationships between the airlines and their passengers.

"An airline can track the profitability of a flight from Dallas to Chicago, but it can't track the Lifetime Value of individual passengers on that flight. Our goal is to help the airlines do exactly that," says Poage.

Poage envisions Sabre helping airlines identify which customers are likely to be traveling with their spouses and might want to spend a long weekend at their destination. Sabre can also identify customers who might respond positively to an offer of extra mileage points in return for taking an earlier or slightly less convenient flight, thereby minimizing the risk of losing those customers to competing carriers.

Armed with this information, the airline can devise travel packages tailored to match a customer's preferences and past decisions.

While several airlines, notably American Airlines and British Airways, are making efforts to achieve this kind of marketing flexibility on their own, all airlines are hampered to a certain extent by their inability to assemble sharply focused customer profiles. The reason is simple: Most passengers don't restrict themselves to a single airline. The airlines also face another obstacle: Historically, frequent flyer programs were designed to reward customers for their loyalty, not necessarily to measure their Lifetime Value. It wasn't until after the programs were in place that airlines realized they could also be used to identify travelers with large Lifetime Value potential.

"That's where we come in," says Poage. "Typically, an airline relies on a handful of outside vendors—Boeing for aircraft, GE for engines, Sperry for avionics—to provide its technology needs. We provide more information technology to the airlines than anyone else. Now our job includes providing the technology that measures Lifetime Value and enables one-to-one marketing."

Sabre has already launched a Web site that could easily

serve as a model for 1to1 marketing of travel services. The site, Travelocity, provides reservation capabilities with more than 420 airlines, 40,000 hotels and 50 rental car companies. Travelocity has signed up more than 4 million members and hopes to have one-to-one relationships with each. "The Web lets a customer take an active role in managing the relationship. The Web makes it easy for customers to tell us about their latest needs and desires. The challenge, of course, is to provide the customer with some quick and tangible benefit in return for interacting with us."

Poage says Sabre has no interest in selling traveler profiles compiled by the Web site. "We are very interested, however, in helping fill their individual unmet needs."

Travelocity also benefits from Sabre's reputation as a vendor of neutral, unbiased information on fares, connections and ancillary services. Poage is hoping the site will emerge as a natural "first stop" for travelers, a sort of Web-based travel agent that can be trusted not only to provide all the information a passenger needs to get from Point A to Point Z but to keep their individual profiles current.

One by-product of the data collected by frequent flyer programs was measurable proof that a handful of any airline's customers generates most of the profits. For the airlines, therefore, it becomes imperative to identify all customers, differentiate them by value to the company, interact with the highest value customers to find out what they want and then customize some aspect of the service to ensure the loyalty of these customers.

Poage offers an example of how this might play out in real life. "Let me compare two travelers. One is a very frequent flyer, the other isn't. Both call an airline to book a seat on the next flight from New York to London. Now, let's say that flight is sold out. The traveler who isn't a frequent flyer will be told just that: The flight is booked solid. The very frequent flyer, on the other hand, will be given a seat. The airline does everything it can to keep that very frequent flyer on board its plane—even if it means offering compensation to another passenger for taking a later flight."

Consider another example in which both callers are frequent flyers, but one caller is clearly identifiable as having greater Lifetime Value than the other. "Let's say we're talking about an 8 A.M. flight from New York to Chicago. The flight has been sold out for weeks. We would find some way to get the high-value traveler on the requested flight. The other caller, who is also a high-volume user, might be offered a seat on a slightly earlier or later flight, along with 500 bonus miles thrown in for free. That way, the customer gets a benefit and the airline still keeps the business."

Because surveys of frequent flyers reveal that the most annoying travel problems occur somewhere in the airport—after stepping out of the taxi but before boarding the plane—Sabre hopes to put its customer knowledge to use in ways that minimize headaches for stressed-out business travelers. High-value customers might be granted access to shorter lines, express services or special transportation. As customer information systems become more integrated and more sophisticated, more decisions affecting customers will be made in real time, closer to the gate, by front-line personnel.

"You have to approach this as a crusade. Every employee has got to internalize it and feel it, because these are behaviors you can't dictate. You can't program the nuances. And the best ideas aren't going to come from the top—they're going to come from your employees and from your customers," says Poage.

"I've always tried to empathize with the people I'm trying to provide services for. I like to talk with customers, meet with them and try to put myself in their shoes. You have to start seeing your services through the eyes of your customers, or you're going to lose them."

Thought Generator
Tool Makers

Never underestimate the value of collective intelligence. Your employees are often your best source of ideas. How well do you harness the creative capacity of your own organization? What would it take to develop a "controlled fusion" process like DoubleClick's? If you had two extra tickets to a "controlled fusion" meeting to give to unlikely candidates, where would you look for them inside your organization?

Are you prepared for an increase in "velocity" within your industry, an unexpected jump in the pace of change? How will you adapt? Whom can you call on to push down on the corporate accelerator?

Are your customers' needs changing, even though they still want the same basic products or services? Can you, in the words of Oracle's Neil Mendelson, "speak to business people about business," instead of focusing just on your own products and services?

What is the true value of the customer information your organization now has? Perhaps, like Sabre, the breadth of the information contains a wealth of value to your channel partners, or to the divisions in your company. How would you even go about calculating how valuable it would be to your firm to be able to see a larger or deeper picture of individual customer relationships?

Please e-mail responses to
toolmakers@1to1.com

Parting Advice

A Letter to Our Readers

Dear Reader:

Change is never easy, and managing the kind of change we've been discussing in this book can be extremely difficult.

Companies don't take naturally to creativity and change, do they? Most companies are already reasonably successful, or they wouldn't exist long enough to reflect on their own strategies. As Descartes might have said if he had been a capitalist, "I profit. Therefore I am." Companies are not designed for change. They are designed to carry on, and the more successful ones are those that carry on more persistently, more relentlessly, more irresistibly.

But now we've heard messages from more than two dozen pioneers exploring a totally new frontier of business activity, an entirely new competitive landscape.

These pioneers are attempting to use newly available technology to apply business principles that, on the surface, make extraordinary sense—developing relationships with individual customers, one customer at a time. "Remembering" a customer from event to event, across different business units and functions. Interacting with and tailoring their company's behavior to the needs of that single, individual, uniquely different customer.

As compelling as they sound, these ideas are deceptively difficult to put into practice. For most firms, they require changing the very nature of the underlying business model.

In our previous books we did our best to catalogue the business principles and competitive issues that characterize this new business model, called customer relationship management, or 1to1 marketing. During our own journey we've noted how the CRM discipline has, over the years, developed into a business model that is more concrete and definable. For example, if you reread *The One to One Future,* our 1993 book that first laid out most of the principles that define CRM today, you'll notice that most business examples in the book are hypothetical. In 1993 it wasn't difficult for us to imagine the way business competition would function in an era of customized production and cost-efficient interactivity, but there were few real-world examples of 1to1 marketing to point to. Instead, we had to validate every new CRM principle with a "what if?" scenario, applied to particular types of businesses, from banks, cars, or diapers, to office supplies, packaged goods, or washing machines.

By 1997, when *Enterprise One to One* was published, there were a number of companies we could write about, particularly in categories like telecom, financial services, and retailing. These firms were pushing the CRM envelope, with reliable, enterprise-wide customer databases and sophisticated customer analysis tools. A number of manufacturers and service organizations had embraced the idea of mass customization. Channel management issues were being faced directly and dealt with in a straightforward, if difficult, way. And by 1997 there was the World Wide Web—that marvelous, new, superbly cost-efficient mechanism for interacting with customers. When *The One to One Fieldbook* appeared in 1999, two years after *Enterprise One to One,* there were already enough companies trying to deal with CRM that we could dedicate an entire book to the mechanics of implementation, without first having to map out the business model and justify it philosophically.

The cases we've documented for you in this book, *The One to One Manager,* are designed to highlight the many ways in which executives at today's companies are trying to embrace the CRM movement, and to examine the problems and obstacles they face. This is still a new territory, largely uncharted. There may be an inevitable logic to the CRM discipline, but the path is certainly not well worn. Not yet, anyway. To apply these commonsense but revolutionary principles, our pioneers must change the way their companies have been organized to carry on with the previous business model.

Our hope is that, armed with the information in this book and its predecessors, you will be able to develop a forceful and convincing case for change at your own enterprise. Use the lessons we've collected in *The One to One Manager* to help manage your company's change process, transforming it into a 1to1 enterprise.

As you develop this vision, you should do some soul searching. Where are you likely to find the greatest resistance to enterprise-wide customer contact and management? How will you defuse, realign, or harness that resistance to keep moving toward your goal? Think about the last time your company faced a major, wrenching change. How did the company and its leadership react? How should they have reacted?

Ask yourself: What are the biggest obstacles to change within your organization? Be honest. Be specific. Identify the people, policies and practices most likely to block the way. Then develop a plan to deal with these obstacles.

Be up front with the people who work with you. Tell them that disrupting complacency is necessary to achieve a culture of service. Tell them it can be confusing and difficult to meld traditional, old-fashioned business ethics, like knowing your customers and treating them as individuals, with advanced technology such as data warehouses, Web applications and digital product configuration.

Tell your people that, while everyone should know where you are headed in the long run, the impact on the company's day-to-day operation can sometimes be inadvertently overlooked. That's okay. It's a necessary risk. Tell your people that mistakes will be tolerated, but resistance will not.

Finally, tell your people you need their help. They have to learn and understand the CRM discipline, the discipline of one-to-one marketing. They must think of ways to help your organization integrate this discipline into its philosophy, its culture, its organizing principles. And they must keep the lines of communication open. Talking about, listening to and dealing with both complaints and praise has never been more important.

Keep in mind as you do all this that few companies fail from catastrophic disasters. Most die by attrition, the "thousand-day disaster." Dragons at the end of the earth do not swallow failing companies whole. They are, instead, nibbled to death by ducks. Creeping commoditization. Margin erosion. Customer defections.

It happens so slowly that few even recognize the danger until it is too late. If you can flag that danger for those you work with, offer them a solution, and then prepare everyone for the journey, you can help your organization survive and prosper. You'll want to tell your people about others who are already making this journey. That's why we wrote *The One to One Manager*—to document the journeys already in process at many different firms, in many different business situations.

We'll be writing more about the challenges facing one-to-one managers in the near future. If you would like to nominate a one-to-one manager to be interviewed for one of our upcoming projects, please contact us. And we'd like very much to hear from *you* as you navigate the 1to1 universe. Remember, you too are a pioneer and a leader. We urge you to share *your* dispatches from the frontier. Send an e-mail to *peppers@1to1.com* or *rogers@1to1.com*. If you don't already subscribe to our free weekly online newsletter, INSIDE 1to1, send an e-mail to *subscribe@1to1.com* so you can start reading about what your colleagues and competitors are doing.

We hope you enjoyed *The One to One Manager*. We're already hard at work on our next book in the series, *The One to One Sales Force*. Like the previous titles, it will deal with the challenges and hurdles faced by organizations moving forward with CRM programs. We will be focusing on such things as automating a sales force, resolving conflicts among sales marketing and customer service, dealing with channel conflicts and compensating a sales force in ways that will leverage the enterprise's customer relationships. If you have a story or anecdote for this new project, or a case study you think is worth documenting for others, please contact us.

If you wish to learn more about customer relationship management and the 1to1 revolution, please visit our Web site, *www.1to1.com*, where you will discover a wealth of useful information, tools, spreadsheets, and case studies. You can also join discussion forums with other 1to1 pioneers and access a directory of vendors. We hope you enjoy your experience there.

All the best,

Don Peppers and Martha Rogers, Ph.D.

Getting Started

If, during the course of reading this book, you found yourself thinking, "I'd really like to be a one-to-one manager, but I just don't know how," then we recommend reading *The One to One Fieldbook*. It's a user-friendly road map to the world of CRM, written specifically to provide readers with step-by-step instructions for developing and sharpening their 1to1 skills. The *Fieldbook* is literally a do-it-yourselfer's manual for starting up and running 1to1 relationship management programs. Nearly half the *Fieldbook* is made up of checklists, worksheets and guided activities designed to facilitate the launch of a 1to1 program, whether this program is a purely tactical, short-term initiative, or part of a broader, more coordinated effort.

Here's an example of an activity from the *Fieldbook* that any manager contemplating a 1to1 program would find highly useful:

A Brainstorming Competition

1. Collect a bright group of managers at your firm from a variety of functions and business units. It is important that all of them be generally familiar with the principles involved in implementing a 1to1 marketing program. It would be best if they've all read at least the first eight chapters in the *Fieldbook*.
2. Divide into teams of no more than three to six people each, and head off into appropriate break-out rooms.

This is a competition, and each team will be trying to outdo the others.

3. Each team, as a team, should give themselves fifteen minutes to write down as many reasons as they can think of to show why making the transition to becoming a 1to1 enterprise will be difficult, or won't work at all, for your organization. Quantity is as important as quality here. You want to uncover every last possible obstacle to making progress.

4. Meet again, as a group, and let each group present its list of obstacles. Organizational barriers, cultural barriers, lack of information, no funding, channel problems, lack of senior management buy-in, an overly resistant sales force—these are the kinds of reasons that should be on everyone's list.

5. Award a prize to the group that came up with the longest list of obstacles. Give another prize to the group that came up with the single best statement of the most insurmountable obstacle.

6. Now collate and consolidate the lists from all the groups, and go over the obstacles one at a time to identify in each case the most cost-efficient, least burdensome way of overcoming it. Will it require a budget? Does the CEO need to weigh in? Do you need a different compensation structure?

7. The result will be an infrastructure "wish list" for your enterprise, and should be incorporated as a part of your transition-planning documentation.

End Notes

The One to One Manager

INTRODUCTION

Page 10: The statistics cited in our discussion about corporate reorganization around customer types were culled from a research report entitled "Managing Customer Relationships," published by The Economist Intelligence Unit in cooperation with Andersen Consulting in October 1998.

Pages 23–24: We conducted an extensive interview with Steve Wiggins, founder and former CEO of Oxford Health Plans, in October 1998 at our Stamford office. Wiggins verified the factual content of our text in March 1999 via e-mail. Oxford Health Plans is a former client of Peppers and Rogers Group.

CHAPTER ONE

Page 30: We heard David Rance, Managing Director of Customer Centricity Ltd, speak at a Chordiant Software event on November 24, 1998. He confirmed the factual accuracy of our text concerning the high cost of customer apathy in June 1999 by e-mail.

Pages 31–38: Our text on First USA was based on information culled from telephone interviews we conducted with First USA CEO Richard Vague in August and September 1998. In them he shared his early work experiences and his insights for developing highly personalized relationships with customers through an innovative program called *At Your Request*. He also spoke at length about the theory and practice of becoming a "trusted agent" in order to nurture profitable customer relationships. Additionally, we spoke with Jocelyn Sutton, senior vice president of marketing at First USA, in November 1998. She confirmed the details of the interviews in April 1999 by e-mail and telephone. First USA is a former client of Peppers and Rogers Group.

Pages 38–45: We interviewed Dr. Paul Otte, president of Franklin University, by telephone in December 1998 about the university's Student Services Associate program and his strategy for treating students like customers to ensure their loyalty. He confirmed the factual content of our text in March 1999 by fax and telephone.

CHAPTER TWO

Pages 51–55: We interviewed John Samuel, managing director of interactive marketing at American Airlines, by telephone in July 1998 about American Airlines' redesigned Web site and personalization efforts. This interview originally appeared in an article that we wrote for the October 1998 issue of *Sales & Marketing Management* magazine entitled "Opening the Door to Customers." American Airlines confirmed the interview by telephone in August 1998 and provided updated information in June 1999.

Pages 53–55: Our observations about the role played by BroadVision in developing the American Airlines site were based largely on our extensive personal knowledge of the company's systems. Peppers and Rogers Group has a significant ongoing business relationship with BroadVision.

Pages 55–57: We interviewed Gustavo Covacevich, *gerente general* of Previnter, by telephone in November 1998. He spoke about the enormous complexities and highly competitive nature of private pension fund plans in Argentina. He also told us about Previnter's use of a relatively inexpensive electronic pocket organizers to capture sales information. He confirmed the details of the interview by fax in March 1999. Peppers and Rogers Group has an ongoing client relationship with Previnter.

Pages 58–71: We interviewed Gordon Shank, chief marketing officer at Levi Strauss, in a series of telephone conversations in September and October 1998 and in February 1999. In the interviews, he recalled his experiences working for Levi Strauss in the 1970s and described the challenges Levi Strauss faced as its customer base matured and new competitors emerged. He told us how, in an effort to capture the next young generation, Levi Strauss set out with a new mass customization strategy that originated with the Personal Pair program and has since evolved into the Original Spin program. Shank confirmed the factual content of our text in February 1999 via fax and telephone. We also spoke with Janie Ligon, vice president Direct to Consumer, in April 1999 about the company's efforts in the consumer direct area. She confirmed the information in June 1999 by telephone. Levi Strauss participated in a research program on the consumer direct channel led by Peppers and Rogers Group in partnership with the Institute of the Future.

Pages 71–76: We interviewed Jim McCann, president and CEO of 1-800-FLOWERS, via e-mail in August 1998. In his written response, he cited the importance of relationship building in his company's core philosophy and the need for technology to create and empower a culture of customer service. Greg Bouris, corporate communications manager at 1-800-FLOWERS, confirmed the factual content of our text via e-mail in March 1999. 1-800-FLOWERS is a current client of Peppers and Rogers Group.

Pages 77–88: We interviewed Jack Antonini, executive vice president of consumer banking at First Union, by telephone in November 1998 about the importance of getting several business units to work together smoothly and seamlessly to provide customers with consistent, predictable service. During these conversations, Antonini led us to his mentor, General Robert McDermott. The two men have established a lasting friendship based on mutual respect and a shared interest in Customer Relationship Management strategies. We also spoke with Anna Marie Thompson, senior vice president, marketing and communications, consumer banking group, in November and December 1999. She confirmed the factual content of our text by e-mail and telephone in January 1999. In addition, we talked to Bob Grignon, senior vice president of policy, planning and analysis for the bank's Deposit, Products and Services division in March 1999. He provided us with essential information about the bank's ATM deposit system. First Union is a former client of Peppers and Rogers Group.

CHAPTER THREE

Pages 92–102: We interviewed General Robert McDermott, the former CEO of USAA, by telephone in December 1998. We discovered highly useful background information on USAA in a September–October 1991 article by Thomas Teal in *Harvard Business Review* entitled "Service Comes First: An Interview with USAA's Robert F. McDermott. We also referenced a July 25, 1988, article in *Forbes* by Toni Mack entitled "They Have the Faith in Us," and a *Fortune Hall of Fame* article from April 4, 1994 that reported the induction of General McDermott into the Fortune Business Hall of Fame. Biographical information also was culled from the 1996 International Insurance Society's Formal Honors Ceremony and Dinner. General McDermott who maintains an excellent library of reference materials, also helped us reconstruct USAA's past. He verified the factual content of our text, as well as adding several key details, in February 1999 by fax and telephone. We also spoke with Paul Ringenbach, a former colleague of General McDermott's at the U.S. Air Force Academy. Ringenbach is the author of a book entitled *USAA: A Tradition of Service, 1922–1997.* He was an associate professor of history at the academy during McDermott's tenure as dean. He later worked at USAA and is considered an expert on the company. Ringenbach offered valuable insight and provided key factual information about USAA policies and procedures. Peppers and Rogers Group has worked with USAA.

Pages 102–108: We interviewed Patrice Listfield, president, information and entertainment services division at SNET, in August 1998 about the company's implementation of the ICEBOX concept to align products with customer groups. We also spoke with Barbara Brown, director human resources at SNET, about the difficulties some managers encountered while trying to lead cross-functional teams. Listfield confirmed the factual content of our text by fax and telephone in January 1999.

Pages 109–111: We spoke with David De Long, a Concord, Mass.-based researcher and consultant and adjunct professor at Boston University's School of Management, several times in January and February 1999 about the challenges encountered by companies when rolling out Customer Relationship Management initiatives. De Long is considered an expert on Change Management issues and was a valuable source of critical insight on a variety of management issues raised in our manuscript. He confirmed the factual content of our text by telephone in February 1999.

CHAPTER FOUR

Page 114: In 1776, Adam Smith wrote about the "division of labor" in *The Wealth of Nations* (Everyman's Library, Alfred A. Knopf, 1991). Smith (1723–1790) is considered the father of modern economics.

Pages 115–121: We interviewed Patrick J. Kennedy, owner of La Mansión del Rio, by telephone in July 1998 about the hotel's use of customer information to lock in loyalty. He also shared valuable insights about Guestnet, La Mansión Hospitality Management Company, and his worldwide campaign to standardize the 1to1 techniques he applies at La Mansión del Rio. He verified the factual content of our text in March 1999 by fax and telephone. Don Peppers is a member of the Guestnet Advisory Board of Directors.

Pages 121–129: We interviewed Anne Lockie, senior vice president and general manager, Saskatchewan, and Shauneen Bruder, senior vice president, market and planning, at Royal Bank of Canada in January 1999. Lockie spoke about the need to consider cultural factors when rolling out a Customer Relationship Management program, noting that no amount of technology can make up for insensitivity on the part of the marketer. Bruder provided technical insight into the statistical models used in the bank's 1to1 initiatives. Lockie confirmed the factual content of our text in February 1999 by fax. Royal Bank of Canada is a former client of Peppers and Rogers Group.

Pages 130–135: We interviewed Steve Wiggins, founder of Oxford Health Plans, in October 1998 at our Stamford office. He shared stories of both his successes and failures at Oxford. He provided us with an extremely valuable firsthand account of Oxford's pioneering efforts in Customer Relationship Management and the perils of trying to grow a business without adequate technology. Wiggins confirmed the information by e-mail on March 3, 1999.

Pages 135–140: We interviewed Brenda French, owner of French Rags, in August 1998. She provided a unique perspective on the importance of pleasing customers and leveraging technology to create innovative products. Her "rags to riches" story demonstrates how an emotional need can be translated, with the help of carefully applied 1to1 techniques, into a significant competitive edge. We also spoke with Richard Haigh, chief operating officer at French Rags, in October 1998. They confirmed the information by e-mail and telephone in March 1999. We also found useful background information about French Rags in a 1995 article by Hal Plotkin that ran in *Inc. Technology,* Issue No. 1, page 62.

Pages 141–143: We interviewed Bruce Varner, fire chief at Carrollton (Texas) Fire Department, in December 1998. Varner's efforts in Carrollton show how an organization can wrap an envelope of personalized care around a basic service. His firefighters not only extinguish blazes, they go the distance to build trusting relationships with the local citizens. He confirmed the information by e-mail in June 1999.

CHAPTER FIVE

Pages 146–152: We interviewed Marc Breslawsky, president of Pitney Bowes, in November 1998. Breslawsky explained how Pitney Bowes has evolved to stay competitive in a world increasingly dominated by fax, e-mail and voice mail. Meredith Fischer, vice president of corporate marketing and chief communications officer at Pitney Bowes, confirmed the information in January 1999 via fax and telephone. Pitney Bowes is a former client of Peppers and Rogers Group.

Pages 152–160: We interviewed Richard Costello, corporate marketing communications manager at General Electric, in November 1998 and Klaus Huber, European sales director, Aircraft Engines division, in December 1998. Both offered valuable insights regarding the advantages of bundling services to increase customer value and loyalty. Costello and Huber explained how programs focused on customer needs are more likely to engender long-term customer loyalty. Bruce Bunch, manager of media relations at GE corporate headquarters, confirmed the factual content of our text in March 1999 by e-mail and telephone.

Pages 161–168: We interviewed Dr. Jim Goodnight, CEO of SAS Institute, in December 1998 about the importance of corporate culture with regard to achieving goals. He also shared firsthand experience about the importance of listening, both to customers and employees. In addition, we spoke with Barrett Joyner, president, SAS Institute North America, Mary Munn, program manager for CFO Vision, Richard Roach, vice president business solutions division, and John McIntyre, director strategic global marketing, in December 1998. Pamela Meek, public relations manager, confirmed the information in January and June 1999 by telephone. Peppers and Rogers Group has worked with SAS Institute.

Pages 169–173: We interviewed Doug Mello, president, Large Business Services–North, Bob Gleason, director of compensation, and Tom Carroll, sales director at Bell Atlantic, in October 1998. Mello shared insights with us regarding the importance of customer service and satisfaction in the overall success equation. He also spoke candidly about the dangers of alienating customers in the midst of making corporate changes. We spoke again with Mello in January 1999. Gleason confirmed the factual accuracy of our text in March 1999 by telephone.

CHAPTER SIX
Pages 178–183: We interviewed Ken Robb, senior vice president of marketing at Dick's Supermarkets, in Febru-

ary 1999 about the importance of using customer data to customize products and services and build relationships with customers. He confirmed the factual content of our text in April 1999 by telephone.

Page 182: The statistics from AC Nielsen's survey were taken from a presentation by John J. Lewis, executive vice president of AC Nielsen, at the AC Nielsen "Category Masters" conference in Scottsdale, Arizona, on September 1, 1998.

Pages 183–187: We interviewed Stephen Cannon, director of marketing at debis Financial Services, in December 1999. He shared the details of the personalized marketing campaigns behind the launch of the Mercedes sport utility vehicle and his consequent relationship-building efforts at debis. He confirmed the information by telephone in April 1999.

Pages 187–192: We interviewed Woody Harford, vice president, business travel marketing, USA, at British Airways in December 1998. He gave us valuable background information about international travelers and told us how British Airways has made great strides using programs such as Venture Club to get, keep and grow customers. Harford confirmed the information in March 1999 by telephone.

Pages 193–195: We interviewed Silvio Bonvini, senior manager of new media, LifeSavers Co., at Nabisco in July 1998 and again in March 1999. Bonvini showed us how with skill, intelligence and sensitivity, organizations can overcome restrictive environments that might prevent less adept competitors from taking full advantage of the World Wide Web. This material originally appeared in an article that we wrote for the October 1998 issue of *Sales & Marketing Management* magazine entitled "Opening the Door to Customers." Bonvini reconfirmed and updated the factual content by telephone in March 1999.

Pages 196–198: We interviewed Katrina Garnett, CEO of CrossWorlds Software, in November 1998. Garnett spoke about the need to differentiate customers and to develop the organizational discipline required to say no to prospects with little strategic value. She also explained the reasons for her decision to hire fashion photographer Richard Avedon to shoot her portrait for a worldwide advertising campaign. Dan Reidy of CrossWorlds' public relations department confirmed and updated the information in June 1999 by telephone.

CHAPTER SEVEN
Pages 203–208: We interviewed Paul Allaire, CEO of Xerox, in November 1998 and Nina Smith, vice president of integrated corporate marketing at Xerox, in November and December 1998. Smith offered a highly detailed picture of the effort at Xerox to expand beyond direct sales while at the same time managing channel conflict issues. Judd Everhart, public relations manager at Xerox, confirmed the details of the interviews by e-mail and telephone in March 1999.

Pages 208–214: We interviewed Shirley Choy-Marshall, marketing program manager at Hewlett-Packard, in March and April 1999. We also spoke with Shen Li, general manager at HP Shopping Village, in April 1999. They explained the reasons behind HP's decision to launch a consumer-oriented Internet store and how the company handled the resulting channel management issues. Li confirmed the information in April 1999 by e-mail and telephone. Peppers and Rogers Group has an ongoing business relationship with Hewlett-Packard.

Pages 214–222: We interviewed Tracy Faleide, general manager of services and sales, and Pam McGee, corporate education specialist at Great Plains Software in January 1999. They detailed for us the critical importance of developing strong relationships with channel partners. Faleide verified the factual content of our text by fax in March 1999. Great Plains Software is a former client of Peppers and Rogers Group.

Chapter Eight
Pages 225–229: We interviewed Kevin O'Connor, CEO of DoubleClick, by telephone in July and August 1998. We also sat in on a brainstorming session he conducted at DoubleClick's New York office. In our conversations, O'Connor stressed the importance of harnessing the collective intelligence around you when considering all the possible uses of technological innovation. He made a strong case for viewing the Internet as an agent of social and historical change. We also spoke with Amy Shapiro, director of corporate communications of DoubleClick, in

July 1998, who explained the company's complicated business model. She confirmed the information in February 1999 by e-mail and telephone. Don Peppers is a member of DoubleClick's board of directors.

Pages 229–233: We interviewed Neil Mendelson, senior director of data warehousing at Oracle, in September and December 1998. He spoke about the transforming effect of technology on business and society at large. As a champion of 1to1 marketing initiatives, Mendelson explained how Oracle was changing to accommodate the customer-oriented needs of its clients. He confirmed the factual content of our text by telephone in March 1999. Peppers and Rogers Group has an ongoing business relationship with Oracle.

Pages 234–239: We interviewed James B. Poage, senior vice president of worldwide marketing at Sabre Travel Information Network, in January 1998. He offered critical insight into the limitations of frequent flyer programs and suggested solutions that would yield a more complete picture of customer needs. He confirmed the information in March 1999 by fax. Peppers and Rogers Group has worked with Sabre.

Index